POWER TO WITNESS

JAMES W. ZACKRISON

D1468625

Pacific Press Publishing Association
Boise, Idaho
Oshawa, Ontario, Canada

Edited by Jerry D. Thomas
Designed by Tim Larson
Cover photos by Betty Blue
Typeset in 10/12 New Century Schoolbook

The author assumes full responsibility for the accuracy of all facts and quotations cited in this book.

Unless otherwise indicated, Scripture references in this book are from the New International Version.

Library of Congress Cataloging-in-Publication Data:

Zackrison, James W., 1932-
    Power to witness : the need of the hour / James W. Zackrison.
      p.   cm.
    Includes bibliographical references.
    ISBN 0-8163-1177-3
    1. Witness bearing (Christianity) 2. Seventh-Day Adventists—
Membership. 3. Adventists—Membership. 4. Sabbatarians—
Membership.   I. Title.
BX6154.Z33   1993
248'.5—dc20   93-24313
                                     CIP

93 94 95 96 97 ● 5 4 3 2 1

Contents

CHAPTER 1

A Real, Live Missionary!

"He's going to say it," my daughter whispered to her brother. "Here it comes," my oldest son whispered back. "Never fails," said our second son to both of them. They waited with bated breath for the announcement, pencils ready!

Sure enough, the man introducing me as the speaker said it exactly as they knew it would happen. "We have with us today Elder Jim Zackrison and his family. They work overseas and they are [there it was] *real, live missionaries!*" Three pencils made quick marks on the ever-present tally sheets. Our three children had been keeping track all during our furlough, and so far they were batting 1.000. Everywhere we went, we were introduced as "real, live missionaries."

It was a joke in our family. "If we're real, 'live' missionaries, are there any real, 'dead' missionaries?" "How about just a plain 'missionary' without the 'live'?" And so it went. Even today, though we no longer work overseas, one of them will make a remark like, "Hey, Dad, how does it feel to be introduced without being either alive or a missionary?"

What is the church for?

When you think about it, though, those people who introduced us as "real, live" missionaries weren't too far off. The church, by its very nature and design in the plan of the Lord, is a living missionary enterprise that takes in the entire population of the world.[1]

Abraham, the first "official" missionary in the Old Testament, was called to be a blessing to *all* the peoples of the earth (see Genesis 12:3). According to this covenant, everyone's birthright resides in the city of God. From the Lord's perspective, even nations like Egypt, Babylon, and Philistia are actually "born" in Jerusalem (Zion—see Psalm 87:5), the Lord's dwelling place and the home of His people, becomes the birthplace, the native city, as it were, of *all* humankind.

In the New Testament, as we will see, the growth of the church and the winning of converts is the focus.

When the time arrives to wind up the great controversy, establish the kingdom, and initiate eternity with new heavens and a new earth (see Revelation 21:1), the Lord sends once again the same message He gave to Abraham and so many others, based on the same covenant and the same target audience: "Then I saw another angel flying in midair, and he had the eternal gospel to *proclaim to those who live on the earth*—to every nation, tribe, language and people" (Revelation 14:6, emphasis mine). The church, regardless of whatever else it may involve itself in, is by nature and configuration a missionary enterprise.

Who gets chosen?

Some people believe that the Lord has already chosen those who will be saved, so we do not really need to seek converts. That, however, is not the message of either the Old or the New Testaments.

For instance, Paul sees civilization itself organized to focus humanity's attention on God:

> From one man he made every nation of men, that they should inhabit the whole earth; and he determined the times set for them and the exact places where they should live. God did this so that men would seek him . . . and find him, though he is not far from each one of us (Acts 17:26, 27).

Ellen White remarks that the Lord set the places people should live in a way that gave them maximum opportunity for close acquaintance with God.[2]

It was always the Lord's plan that Israel would act as a mission agency to spread the good news. "The Lord will have compassion on Jacob; once again he will choose Israel and will settle them in their own land. Aliens will join them and unite with the house of Jacob" (Isaiah 14:1).

A key Messianic passage indicates that the coming Messiah would be sent to all nations: "Here is my servant, whom I uphold, my chosen one in whom I delight; I will put my Spirit on him and he will bring justice to the nations" (Isaiah 42:1) (see Matthew 12:18).

According to the Scriptures, then, the Lord calls everyone. But the calling is done through us. We are His voice.

Jesus—a real, live missionary

Jesus was a great missionary, though He never crossed saltwater and He never left the boundaries of His home region.

When Simeon the priest blessed the Baby Jesus, he specifically said that He would be a "light for revelation to the Gentiles" (Luke 2:32). In other words, the message of Jesus' role in the plan of salvation was intended to go to everyone.

As his message developed, it became increasingly clear that it was urgent and destined for all the world. For instance, in the writings of John, there are eight instances where Jesus is directly called the Saviour of the *world* (see chart).

Text	Statement	Event
1 John 2:2	An atoning sacrifice for the whole world	John's personal viewpoint
1 John 4:14	We have seen and testify	John's view built on personal experience and observation

Text	Statement	Event
John 1:29	"The Lamb of God who takes away the sin of the world."	Baptism. Announced at the very start of Jesus' ministry
John 3:17	God sent His Son to save the world	Discussion with Nicodemus
John 4:42	"We know that this man really is the Savior of the world"	Men of Sychar— Samaritans
John 6:51a	"I am the living bread . . . which I will give for the life of the world."	Discourse on the bread of life in Galilee
John 12:31	"I . . . will draw all men to myself"	Passion week. Discourse on His death and the reasons for it
John 17; 20:21	"Let the world know that you sent me."	Jesus' prayer for Himself, the disciples, and all believers

How urgent is soul winning?

Two major events mark the agricultural year in Palestine—the early and the latter rain. The early rain germinates the seed, and the latter rain ripens the harvest. The Bible writers use this terminology to symbolize the span of time between the Day of Pentecost, recorded in Acts 1, and the events leading up to the second coming of Jesus. You will immediately recognize that this is also "Adventist vocabulary." Students of prophecy, Adventists included, have written volumes about when the "latter rain" will fall and what will happen. Overly enthusiastic preachers often point to spectacular current events as marking the beginning of the latter rain. Critics of the church frequently claim they will be among the first to receive the latter rain, though no one else apparently will know about it.

Jesus, however, used the symbolism in a unique way. In John 4, He points out to the disciples that though they know how to calculate correctly the time between the two rains ("Do you not say 'Four months more and then the harvest'?"), they overlooked the fact that through Jesus' eyes the fields are *already ripe* for the harvest, even before the latter rain came (see John 4:35). The point is that there are people out there just waiting for the good news, just like the Samaritan woman Jesus found at Jacob's well. The problem is the lack of harvesters to get the people!

The disciples had no church-growth eyes. They didn't "see" any Samaritans ready to harvest. Jesus saw whole villages of them. People just waiting to be "seen" also fill the city, town, or village where you live!

Forceful advance by forceful people

To Jesus, this is an urgent concern. Matthew 11:12 is another frequently overlooked text illustrating the urgency of getting the message out:

> From the days of John the Baptist until now, the kingdom of heaven has been forcefully advancing, and forceful men lay hold of it.

There is a discussion about exactly how the Greek grammar of this text reads, but it seems to be what is called a "middle" voice in Greek. You will notice that your King James Version reads, "And from the days of John the Baptist until now the kingdom of heaven suffereth violence, and the violent take it by force." It interprets the Greek as a passive voice, making it sound like the kingdom itself is being persecuted. More up-to-date translations, however, choose the middle voice. In this case, it is the kingdom that is taking the world by storm, and "forceful" people—bold, dedicated disciples—are getting the message out (see Luke 16:16). One translator puts it this way: "From the days of John the Baptist until now, the kingdom of God is applying violent pressure, and the courageous are seizing it for themselves."[3]

What does that have to do with you and me? Listen to what one modern writer says about "forceful" witnessing:

> Don't listen to your physical symptoms, or your physical responses to fear. You might be shaking in your boots, you might stumble over your words, your mouth might be dry as cotton, you might sweat, or you might cry. There are all kinds of things you might do, but if you say, 'I don't care what I am physically going through, I am not going to allow that to stop me, I am going to help people,' that fear will leave. If you step out in faith, and in obedience to what God has told you to do, you will be victorious the way He says you will. When you act in love, fear cannot remain.[4]

When it comes down to it, you can't doze your way into the kingdom! Ellen White puts it on the line when she says, referring to Matthew 11:12:

> With the great truth we have been privileged to receive, we should, and under the Holy Spirit's power we could, become living channels of light. We could then approach the mercy seat; and seeing the bow of promise, kneel with contrite hearts, and seek the kingdom of heaven with a spiritual violence that would bring its own reward. We would take it by force, as did Jacob. Then our message would be the power of God unto salvation.[5]

Two basic methods

The Bible outlines two basic methods of getting the message out and winning converts. One works from the outside in and the other from the inside out. The first method was used extensively during Old Testament times; the second from the time of the New Testament until today. Both are valuable, but the latter is more effective today.

Why the queen of Sheba went to church

In Old Testament times, the plan was for the people groups around the nation of Israel to observe how well-organized and progressive the nation was. Then they would make a trip to Jerusalem to see why all these good things were happening. Once they got there, someone would take them to church (see Deuteronomy 4:5-8).

That is what Solomon did with the queen of Sheba (see 1 Kings 10). She made the trip, she said, because she "heard about the fame of Solomon and his relation to the name of the Lord," and wanted to "test him with hard questions" (verse 1). Solomon showed her "the burnt offerings he made at the temple of the Lord," and "she was overwhelmed" (verse 5). As a result, she went away with a bright picture of the Lord and what He can do for people.

> Praise be to the Lord your God, who has delighted in you and placed you on the throne of Israel. Because of the Lord's eternal love for Israel, he has made you king, to maintain justice and righteousness (1 Kings 10:9).

Centuries later, one of her countrymen would find the connection between the Jewish religion and Christianity through a missionary he met on a desert road (Acts 8:26-40).[6]

This system of outreach has a fancy name: "centripetal." That means that you stand in one place, and people come to you. For instance, Isaiah said, "The mountain of the Lord's temple will be established as chief among the mountains; . . . and all nations will stream to it" (Isaiah 2:2). Read the whole chapter for details on how the system was supposed to work.

"So send I you"

In the New Testament, things changed. Jesus took a different approach. He advocated a "sending" message. He said things like, "As the Father has sent me, I am sending you" (John 20:21).

Ellen White writes:

> The gospel commission is the great missionary charter of Christ's kingdom. The disciples were to work earnestly

for souls, giving to all the invitation of mercy. They were not to wait for the people to come to them; they were to go to the people with their message.[7]

The system was no longer centripetal. It was now "centrifugal," that is, it flew out from a center. It no longer sucked people in; it shot them out to find other people to bring in. The following diagram shows how the two systems work.

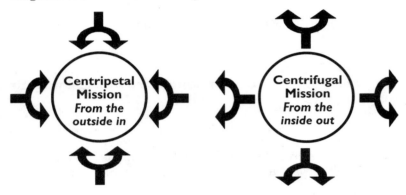

The centrifugal mission system outlined in the New Testament is the reason Jesus said the kingdom was moving "forcefully." New Testament disciples are more than spectators, as we will learn in the next chapter. In today's world, it doesn't do much good to stand on a street corner somewhere, as it were, and "shine." We usually call it "setting a good example." That is valuable, but it is not enough. You will be there a long time before anyone takes the time to ask you why you are standing there shining. Besides, this shining-saint idea all too often gives birth to the Great Saint syndrome that Isaiah described. It afflicts people who say, "Keep away; don't come near me, for I am too sacred for you" (Isaiah 65:5).

Real disciples become soldiers in the Lord's army. The church becomes militant. It is clothed in the gospel armor (see Ephesians 6:11). It starts to march and "battle." Jesus no longer hangs on a cross; He rides on a white horse, swinging a sword and dressed in battle gear (see Revelation 19). When the judgment starts, little horns and big horns who ran roughshod over the saints for centuries are suddenly brought up short because God's throne starts to blaze, and rivers of fire flow out (see Daniel 7:9, 10). Blazing chariot wheels take off after the enemies of God, and they meet a well-deserved end. The people of God get the sovereignty, power, and greatness handed over to them (see Daniel 7:27).

So you and I, out there in our various churches and homes, are handed a message from three angels racing to beat the clock. A message that says, " 'Fear God and give glory to him, for the hour of his judgment has come' " (Revelation 14:7). Those angels shout and blow trumpets to get people's attention, but they don't preach. They empower *us* to preach and teach.

Sinners come in all sizes and shapes

Flying angels often bump into stone walls disguised as people with stony personalities. Sometimes they bump into stained-glass barriers inside the church itself. Jesus said in Matthew 13:1-23 that they, and you and I, will meet some people who are tough as the impenetrable soil on the side of the path, a few who are hard as rock, some with thorny personalities, and, fortunately, more than a few who are "good ground."

It takes the right kind of method to reach each category. We will learn more about this later in this book. For now, suffice to say that Jesus Himself used different approaches, even though He had a master method that we will learn about in chapter 4. Notice some of the illustrations Jesus used.

Symbol	Text	Soul-Winning Principle
Two by two to face the wolves	Luke 10:1-3	Jesus sent the disciples out two by two with a warning about "wolves."
Lost sheep	Luke 15:1-7	Lost sheep rarely find their way back without help.

Symbol	Text	Soul-Winning Principle
Lost coins	Luke 15:8-10	Lost coins don't even know they are lost.
Lost sons	Luke 15:11-23	Some people hit bottom before they know they are lost.
Lost older brothers	Luke 15:25-31	Some people in the church don't know their real condition.

Making headlines in heaven

As we have seen, the purpose of the church is to grow. It does not exist for itself, but only to fulfill a mission. The minute the church loses sight of that mission, it becomes just another social entity among many. The church may do other things on occasion, and individual, local congregations may go about growing using various methods, but the mandate does not change. Everything is secondary to its main function—to grow.

What does "to grow" mean? Here is a working definition:

For a church to grow means that it will grow consistently in three areas: the number of converts it wins, growth of the spirituality of its members, and the multiplication of ministries it carries out.

The church makes headlines in heaven when it does that job: "I tell you that in the same way there is more rejoicing in heaven over one sinner that repents than over ninety-nine righteous persons who do not need to repent" (Luke 15:7). "There is rejoicing in the presence of the angels of God over one sinner who repents" (Luke 15:10).

Before too long, those saved people, the angels, and everyone else in heaven are going to get together as a great multitude too numerous to count and shout a song of praise to the One who made it all possible:

> And they cried out in a loud voice: "Salvation belongs to our God, who sits on the throne, and to the Lamb" (Revelation 7:10).

We members are the newsmakers and the movers and shakers of the church. We make daily decisions whether we will be headlines in heaven or buried on the back page somewhere. We are the real, live missionaries who make it happen. So hit the streets, Adventists. The hour of His judgment *is here*!

---

1. There are people who believe that all religions have some good in them and that any religion leads to salvation. That theory is not upheld by the Bible. See John 1:1-9.

2. *The Acts of the Apostles*, 238. The ramifications of what this verse means are beyond the scope of this book. Ellen White's statement should not be taken to mean that contemporary political boundaries are set by God. There have been Adventists who believed this, but it is not Paul's or Ellen White's meaning.

3. Max Meinertz, *Teologia del Nuevo Testamento* (Madrid: Ediciones Fax, 1956), 34, 121.

4. Wendy Treat, *Bold, Effective, Fearless Witnessing* (Seattle: Christian Faith Center), 10.

5. *SDA Bible Commentary*, 5:1089.

6. Read the story in a church-history book of the development of Christianity in Ethiopia. Early Adventist missionaries found there a style of Christianity incorporating much of what we believe and teach.

7. *The Acts of the Apostles*, 28.

CHAPTER 2

Discipleship Is a Verb

"That's what we pay you for!"

A friend of mine recently began reorganizing his congregation around a plan based on the New Testament. One of his first steps was to preach a series of sermons on discipleship. His point was that according to the New Testament, the main job of a congregation is to win souls and grow and that everyone should be involved.

He didn't get far, however, until a significant number of church members—yes, we're talking about an Adventist church here—almost literally rebelled. "That," they said, "is what we pay *you* for. Our job as church members is to come and hear you preach and keep the church looking nice." Who's correct here, the people or the pastor?

To answer that question, we have to take a look at the meaning and use of the word *disciple* in the Bible, how it combines with the word *apostle*, and how the two merge into an action word, *discipleship.*

The original disciples

We all know about Jesus' twelve disciples. Peter is the most famous; Philip and Nathanael are seldom heard of. James the son of Alphaeus, Thaddaeus, and Simon the Zealot are unknown except as names to memorize. Judas Iscariot is famous as a traitor. James and John are remembered for their bad tempers and political maneuvers (see Mark 3:17; Matthew 20:20-24). Thomas is recognized as the one who wanted proof for everything (see John 20:24-28). The Roman Catholic Church has even taken Peter and turned him into the first pope and the "rock" to which their church is anchored!

These twelve people are usually understood to be *the* disciples of Jesus. They were eyewitnesses to the events of His ministry, and some of them became authors of parts of the New Testament.

Is anyone else a disciple?

This raises the question of whether the word *disciple* is restricted to these twelve men. *Disciple* is the English equivalent of the Greek word for a learner or a student, usually with the idea that the person adheres to a specific teacher. For instance, the Pharisees claimed to be disciples of Moses (see John 9:28), and they themselves had disciples (see Matthew 22:16). Actually, *disciple* is a common designation for all followers of the Lord (see Acts 18:23). Any person, then, who believes on Jesus and becomes an adherent to Christianity is designated a disciple.

Who are the disciples in your church?

Peter, who of all people ought to know who disciples are, says that the people of God are:

> Living stones, . . . being built into a spiritual . . . priesthood, offering spiritual sacrifices acceptable to God through Jesus Christ. . . . A chosen people, a royal priesthood, a holy nation, a people belonging to God, that you may declare the praises of him who called you out of darkness into his wonderful light (1 Peter 2:5, 9).

According to Peter, then, there is no such thing as a church member who *isn't* a disciple. It comes with the package! When you are born again, you are designated a disciple, and, as we will see shortly, you are also designated an apostle, because you are automatically given a commission to "go." The only way you cannot be a disciple is to openly refuse to be one. Ellen White puts it this way: "Every true disciple is born into the kingdom of God as a missionary."[1]

This concept of discipleship is nothing new. Peter picked this text up from Exodus 19, and the same dynamic was true in Old Testament times. Exodus 19:6 says that *all* Israelites were designated as part of a kingdom of priests. The reason they were all "priests" is because they were supposed to be a missionary nation and take the knowledge of the Lord to all people groups.[2] It is true that in the Israelite sanctuary and temple services, the Levites were given special duties and assignments (see Numbers 1:47-53). However, they were never designated as a special social class or separated spiritually from the rest of the nation. The Lord never instituted any distinction between clergy and laity as we often perceive it today.

What is a disciple?

More precisely, then, *what* is a disciple? What turned fishermen and tax collectors into disciples?

We usually think of Jesus' disciples as rather poor, unsophisticated rural types out of the backwoods of Galilee. Is that really true? Peter and his family owned a fair-sized fishing business. We would call them small businesspeople today. Peter was also pretty efficient in martial arts. How many people can aim a sword with enough accuracy to get just an ear, not the rest of someone's head! Matthew was a Roman government civil-service employee making a good salary (plus skimming some off the top now and again and extorting as much as possible).[3] Simon the Zealot was a political activist, well versed in the ins and outs of political intrigue. Judas, though he was a subversive and a crook, was certainly highly intelligent.

Looking at it from a human standpoint, the original twelve made considerable personal sacrifices to leave their accustomed lifestyles to trek around the country with an itinerant preacher and healer. So, being a disciple implies an intentional commitment. Jesus called it "taking up your cross" (see Luke 14:25-34). Discipleship does not come cheap.

The interface between *disciple* and *apostle*

Mark 3:14 says that when Jesus chose these twelve men to

be His disciples, He also designated them as apostles.

As we have noted, the word *disciple* refers to a student, a learner. *Apostle*, on the other hand, refers to someone who is sent on a mission. Jesus called the twelve, Mark notes, "that they might be with him [disciples], *and* that he might send them out to preach [apostles]."

We have two things here. One is the learning aspect. You cannot do an adequate job of anything for the kingdom of God unless you know what you are doing. Too many of us church members tend to function on the basis of tradition rather than biblical teaching and slogans rather than biblical knowledge.

Nevertheless, learning about the kingdom is not an end in itself. It is only half the job a person takes on when he or she commits to the Lord. The other half is the "sending." Too many church congregations are made up of a collection of individuals who congregate under one roof on Sabbath morning for a couple of hours but are in no way a "body." They simply arrive and go away again. Nothing happens to advance the kingdom! Arriving and going back home is not a response to the "sending" message of the New Testament. "Coming in" for personal spiritual benefit has to be balanced with "going out" to share the benefits with someone else.

Is anyone else an apostle?

Were the original twelve the only "sent ones"? We tend to perceive the word *apostle* as indicating a position in a hierarchy. Because of that connotation, many people believe that apostleship ended when the original twelve, plus Paul, died. Others apply the word only to certain church officials, a concept known as apostolic succession. The Roman Catholic Church, for instance, believes that each succeeding pope is a direct recipient of the authority of the original apostles, especially Peter. Some other denominations, such as the Anglican and Episcopal churches, believe that all bishops ordained by the laying on of hands are given apostolic powers akin to those of the original apostles.[4]

In the New Testament, however, a whole array of people are designated apostles. Paul, Barnabas (see Acts 14:14), and even relatively unknown people like Andronicus and Junia (see Romans 16:7), a couple of Paul's relatives, are all called apostles.

Paul vigorously defends his right to be called an apostle based on having seen the Lord in vision (see 1 Corinthians 9:1), having received a direct call from the Lord (see Acts 9), and being appointed by the Lord (see 1 Timothy 2:7). The list of spiritual gifts in Ephesians 4:11 indicates that other people are also called to be apostles. We have already seen how Peter put the two concepts together in 1 Peter 2:5.

The great commission and discipleship

In the great commission, recorded in Matthew 28:16-20, turning people into disciples becomes a command and is interfaced with a sending message.[5] "Therefore go," Jesus said, "and make disciples of all nations." Your King James Version says "teach all nations," but the actual construction in the original Greek means "make disciples." This brings in the aspect of disciple*ship*, how being a disciple combines with being sent and then transfers into everyday Christian life.

There are four elements mentioned by Jesus is this passage:

1. Go.
2. Make disciples.
3. Baptize them.
4. Teach them to obey everything I have commanded you.

These four elements set up a two-step process by which the church is supposed to work.

Baptize them

Go

Make disciples

Teach them

The first step in the process is the "going." The church is called to go—the centrifugal mission system we talked about in the previous chapter. Going is a fundamental aspect of church life. As Ellen White puts it: "The very life of the church depends upon her faithfulness in fulfilling the Lord's commission."[6] The second step is a combination of making disciples, baptizing, and teaching.[7]

We Adventists traditionally make an arbitrary division of church life into "nurture" and "outreach." There is no such distinction in the Bible. When we do that, we disrupt the process of making disciples and leave it unfinished. That is why we so often hear complaints from new converts that they were visited and studied with until they were baptized. Then they were summarily "dumped" into the congregation and pretty much left to sink or swim on their own. Lots of church back doors swing open on these artificially created hinges![8]

The same goes for arbitrarily dividing evangelism into "public" and "personal." There is no such distinction in the Bible. Whether the group you are addressing is large or small, the dynamic of making disciples is the same.

This has gotten so far out of hand in Adventist circles that the word *evangelism* only means to many of us "public meetings," an unfortunate limiting of a dynamic biblical concept to only one strategy.[9]

Constantine messes up the church

It was the Emperor Constantine, around A.D. 300, who muddled up the concept of discipleship, just as he and his half-Christian cohorts threw a monkey wrench into the church machinery and fooled around with the Sabbath and a cluster of other biblical beliefs.

Here's how it happened. There were no church buildings to speak of up to that time. People met in homes and ran their own meetings, usually led by elders, also called bishops. Some of these elders became sort of unofficial clergy, but they were still just members of local congregations, recognized for their spiritual gifts of leadership.[10] Constantine allowed an assortment of former pagan priests to become pastors of Christian groups.

Ornate pagan temples became Christian churches, and gaudy pagan ceremonies were converted into Christian ceremonies, often with very little, if any, change, except to modify some names and read from the Bible instead of a pagan book.

What Constantine and his cohorts actually did was to set up a hierarchy and distinction between clergy and nonclergy. Clergy led out in church, and nonclergy became pew potatoes. Discipleship, active participation in the advancement of the kingdom, came to a screeching halt.

Things are not much different today. Someone said that an average church service is a lot like a football game. Thousands of people in the stands who desperately need exercise are watching eleven people on the field who desperately need rest! For instance, the average church pastor will preach two thousand sermons over his lifetime. The average church member will preach none. Where do you find that in the Bible?

The priesthood of all believers

As time went by, Constantine's organizational system produced a marked distinction between clergy and laity. The word *laity*, as we understand it today, appeared in church vocabulary during the Middle Ages. It comes from the Latin word *laicus*, derived from the Greek word *laos*, which means "people." It came to be used in contrast to *clericus*, referring to the official priesthood during that time. For instance, Gratian, known as the father of canon law in the Roman Catholic Church, said that there are actually two kinds of Christians, lay or secular, and clergy.[11] Stephen of Tournai (died 1203) added that there were lower people (the laity) and higher people (the clergy), each with a different reward in heaven.[12]

Martin Luther was one of the first to realize this wasn't true, and it changed his life. In his day, almost everyone in the Western Christian world was a Roman Catholic and was taught that official, ordained clergy were special people with special contact with God. You could only get to God through your parish priest.

Luther discovered that before God, we are all "priests." This concept is known in Christian theology as the priesthood of all believers. Today, we use the word *discipleship* as a synonym for the priesthood of all believers, with some added information on how it works out in everyday church life.

Tools for discipleship

Disciples are not left without tools with which to do the work. The primary tools are called spiritual gifts. They are listed in three places in the New Testament: Romans 12:6-8; 1 Corinthians 12:7-11; and Ephesians 4:11. Suffice it to say that it is through the functions of these gifts that discipleship turns from a noun into a verb, from a concept into action.

Defining discipleship

We are now ready for a concise definition of discipleship based on the descriptions we have studied and the interface between being called and being sent:

> A disciple is a person who has been born again, joined the church, identified his or her spiritual gifts, accepted a role in the church compatible with those gifts, and is committed to fulfilling that role *without continual external motivation.*

That is the call and commission every Christian receives, and a committed disciple does it because he or she loves the Lord. No one has to put a guilt trip on committed disciples to get them to church. No one has to call them on the phone every week to get them out of bed on Sabbath morning. No one has to . . . you finish the sentence!

The call, the commissioning, and the sending command all come with the new-birth experience and are designed to be an integral part of every Christian's lifestyle.

The congregation mentioned at the beginning would apparently be happy with Emperor Constantine as their pastor. Real discipleship, on the other hand, is not just an idea, it is a verb, it is action, it is giving the gospel some feet—your feet!

1. *The Desire of Ages*, 195.
2. If you are interested in a detailed analysis of this point, read Johannes Blauw, *The Missionary Nature of the Church* (New York: McGraw-Hill, 1962).
3. If you want to know more about how these people operated, look up *Publican* in the *SDA Bible Dictionary*. Some indication of how well they did is Zacchaeus's statement that he would pay back *four times* what he stole. Maybe that was his extorted profit (see Luke 19:8).
4. You can read about this issue in any dictionary of theology, for instance, *Evangelical Dictionary of Theology* (Grand Rapids, Mich.: Baker Book House, 1984), 73. Seventh-day Adventists believe that the real authoritative successor to the apostles is the New Testament itself. As the great commission says, "Teaching them to obey everything I have commanded you."
5. This commission is repeated in each Gospel with a different emphasis. See Mark 16:14-20; Luke 24:44-49; and John 20:19-23. We will refer to some of these in various chapters in this book.
6. *The Desire of Ages*, 825.
7. There has been some discussion over whether these three things happen one after the other or if they are a combined process. A scholar named Dennis Oliver wrote a doctoral dissertation that adequately proves that this is a combined process rather than a sequence of events and decisions. (Dennis Oliver, "Make Disciples" [Doctor of Missiology diss., Fuller Theological Seminar, 1973]).
8. If you are interested in how you can build a church organizational plan that puts all these elements together, get a booklet titled *How to Set Up and Run an Evangelization / Assimilation Cycle in Your Church* from the North American Division Distribution Center in Lincoln, Nebraska.
9. Please don't take this to mean a depreciation of public evangelism. I am trying to separate biblical categories from contemporary methodologies so we can get our priorities straight. Public evangelism is a fine strategy, but one strategy does not encompass the full meaning of "make disciples."
10. Even in New Testament times a few of them got out of hand and took too much authority on themselves. See 3 John 9, 10.
11. Gratian was an Italian monk who died in A.D. 1160. See *The New International Dictionary of the Christian Church* (Grand Rapids, Mich.: Zondervan, 1974), s.v. "Gratian."
12. Gottfried Oosterwal, *Mission: Possible* (Nashville: Southern Publishing Association, 1972), 105.

CHAPTER 3

Is the Holy Spirit a Pentecostal?

The preacher started out fairly sedately. He had a good text and a heartfelt appeal to the congregation.

It wasn't long, though, before things started to get fired up. He recounted how he had been rescued by the Holy Spirit from an unemotional, unspiritual pulpit and had gotten the Spirit in a miraculous way. A new light came into his eyes, and they started to sparkle. Then he jumped up and down. His hair waved here and there. He leapt up on a table on the stage and bounced off again.

I watched one of the men on the platform. At first he listened intently. Then I noticed he was getting edgy. He shifted on the edge of his seat. Then he almost slid off onto the floor. Suddenly he leapt up in rhythm with the preacher and launched into a sermon of his own, but in an unknown tongue.

That set the congregation off. Suddenly, it was total pandemonium, at least to me, a sedate member of an even more sedate institutional Adventist church where the only person I ever saw even slide around on a pew was the organist when he got excited about some Bach counterpoint he was playing, and then it wasn't much of a slide!

I had never been in a Pentecostal church before. I was there doing a class assignment on worship services, and to me, it was really something else.

Then it got scary. All of a sudden someone in the congregation got a message "in the Spirit" that there was a person present who was not a believer, and a bunch of people looked right at me.

I wasn't sure what kind of a nonbeliever they had in mind, but the hair started to stand out on my neck. I decided it was time to leave. Enough already!

I have been in many Pentecostal services since then and have good friends in Pentecostal circles. Some of the services I have attended have been about the same as any Adventist worship service. One of my friends said about his church, "Our worship services have two distinguishing marks: Everyone comes in late, and they all sit in the back!" I can identify with that!

Some services have been stunning, in a good way, like the one my wife and I attended at the largest church in the world, in Seoul, Korea. An absolutely marvelous worship experience with no hint of the goings-on at the church where I had my initiation, although both belong to the same denomination.

I relate these experiences because when the Holy Spirit, and especially the power of the Holy Spirit, is mentioned in Adventist circles, these seem to be the images that immediately pop up. We seem to have conditioned ourselves to relate the mere mention of the power of the Holy Spirit with Pentecostals.

The Holy Spirit is not a Pentecostal

The Holy Spirit, however, is not a Pentecostal. He was around long before any Pentecostals came into being.

It was the Holy Spirit who "hovered over the waters" during Creation week (see Genesis 1:2) and who contended with humanity for 120 years before the Flood (see Genesis 6:1-3). It was the Holy Spirit who "filled" John the Baptist from the moment of his birth (see Luke 1:15). The Holy Spirit energized and launched the early church (see Acts 1:8), and it is the Holy Spirit who pulls it all together at the end time and gets the church ready for the second advent (see Joel 2:28-32).

We cannot allow our personal reactions to a modern-day phenomenon like Pentecostalism to so prejudice our minds that we allow ourselves to be robbed of the power of heaven available to all Christians, and by doing so lose the blessing the Lord has in store.

Last-day expectations in Adventist eschatology

We Adventists have a marked tendency to think of the actions of the Holy Spirit as primarily related to two historical events, the early and the latter rain. On a diagram, it looks like this:

**The Adventist Perspective
on the Role of the Holy Spirit**

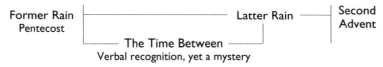

The problem is that we tend to focus on these two events and ignore the power and working of the Holy Spirit on a day-to-day basis during the time in between, except to give it a kind of verbal recognition.

For instance, after giving a series of lectures on the Holy Spirit at Adventist colleges and churches, one writer says:

> I was struck (and depressed) by the extent to which loyal, committed Christians saw the Holy Spirit as an enigma, a stranger, and, to a large extent, Someone yet to come.[1]

Ellen White recorded the same concern over a hundred years ago (1891). This quotation is a little long, but it is extremely important:

> Just prior to His leaving His disciples for the heavenly courts, Jesus encouraged them with the promise of the Holy Spirit. *This promise belongs as much to us as it did to them, and yet how rarely it is presented before the people*, and its reception spoken of in the church. In consequence of this silence upon this most important theme, *what promise do we know less about by its practical fulfillment than this rich promise of the gift of the Holy Spirit*, whereby efficiency is to be given to all our spiritual labor? The

promise of the Holy Spirit is casually brought into our discourses, is incidentally touched upon, and that is all. Prophecies have been dwelt upon, doctrines have been expounded; *but that which is essential to the church in order that they may grow in spiritual strength and efficiency, in order that the preaching may carry conviction with it, and souls be converted to God, has been largely left out* of ministerial effort. This subject has been set aside, as if some time in the future would be given to its consideration. Other blessings and privileges have been presented before the people until a desire has been awakened in the church for the attainment of the blessing promised of God; *but the impression concerning the Holy Spirit has been that this gift is not for the church now, but that at some time in the future it would be necessary for the church to receive it.*[2]

She adds that "this promised blessing, if claimed by faith, *would bring all other blessings in its train."*[3]

In order to get over this hump, we need to understand three things:

1. The role the Holy Spirit played in the former rain.
2. The role the Holy Spirit plays in the latter rain.
3. The role the Holy Spirit plays in between these two events.

What did the Holy Spirit do in the early church?

This is the period that falls under the time of the early rain of the Holy Spirit. During this period the Holy Spirit gave people the instantaneous ability to converse in languages not their own (see Acts 2:4).[4] He turned frightened disciples into bold preachers (see Acts 4:3), directly indicated certain people for certain missions (see Acts 13:2), solved doctrinal problems in a specific way (see Acts 15:28), prohibited missionaries from entering certain areas (see Acts 16:6), directed them to other areas (see Acts 16:10), and was the power behind all kinds of miracles and extraordinary happenings (see Acts 19).

Besides that, the Holy Spirit appears in the early church period as the enlightener of Christian minds (see 1 Corinthians 2:6-16) and the sealing agent, the authenticator, as it were, of personal Christian experience (see Ephesians 4:30).

Turning the Spirit loose in Ephesus

What happened in the city of Ephesus, recorded in Acts 19, is an example. Paul discovered a small group of twelve disciples there. Followers of John the Baptist, they could have been in Ephesus for as long as ten years. They had never heard of the Holy Spirit, and their impact on the city was nil.

Once the Holy Spirit got hold of them, however, things began to move. Extraordinary miracles happened. People got well, evil spirits, some of the disarmed elemental spirits of the world Paul talks about, got bumped, and within two years the Christian message was well-known in the city and surrounding provinces (see Acts 19:10). Finally, Christianity became so powerful that it cut into the profits of the idol-makers' market and caused a riot in the city.

So when was the last time your church caused a riot? Enough said!

The Holy Spirit is not a formula

Some Jewish exorcists felt the power and decided to buy in. It didn't work. They thought the Holy Spirit was a formula. " 'In the name of Jesus, whom Paul preaches, I command you to come out' " (Acts 19:13). This is precisely where the charismatic movement all too often separates from the biblical truth of the Holy Spirit. By substituting a subjective experience for objective Bible truth, however unwittingly, the Holy Spirit is converted into a tool of the people rather than the heaven-appointed administrator of the church.[5]

In the case of these seven exorcists, the formula didn't work. " 'Jesus I know,' " the evil spirit answered, " 'and Paul I know, but who are you?' " Now things got real. "The evil spirit jumped on them and overpowered them all. He gave them such a beating that they ran out of the house naked and bleeding" (Acts 19:16). When anyone takes on the devil while still functioning under the devil's banner, they are in for trouble. They always lose. Do the same thing under the Lord's banner, and you always win.

What happens during the latter rain?

Most Adventist writing and discussion about the latter rain focuses on preparation for it. We are very much into personal piety. That, of course, is certainly a worthy concern, and merits unceasing study and everyday application to our individual lives.

Nevertheless, Ellen White gives us some insights into how the Holy Spirit will also intervene in society in general and what will happen during this period. Our main source of information is *The Great Controversy*, pages 611, 612. There's also an application to personal preparation recorded in *Testimonies to Ministers*, pages 506-512.

The latter rain is interfaced with the appearance of the angel mentioned in Revelation 18:1 (see *The Great Controversy*, p. 611). That angel takes on "Babylon" in a face-to-face confrontation over Babylon's belief system and influence, called the "maddening wine of her adulteries" (Revelation 18:3). The controlling influences in Babylon are precisely those mentioned by Paul as the "powers." "She has become," John writes, "a home for demons and a haunt for every evil spirit, a haunt for every unclean and detestable bird" (Revelation 18:2).

This is where the action begins. The angel pops onto the scene with great authority, illuminates the earth with his glory, and shouts with a mighty voice (see Revelation 18:1). According to Ellen White, there will be miracles, healings, and signs and wonders done by church members (see Mark 16:14-20).[6] At the same time, the events are connected with a massive diffusion of the theological message of the third angel in Revelation 16:9-11.[7]

What occurs is that the energy generated by the Holy Spirit, which Ellen White terms "a special bestowal of spiritual grace," and "in a special sense the heavenly gift . . . sought and found," energizes church members and motivates them to hit the streets.[8] Here is a description:

The message will be carried not so much by argument as

by the deep conviction of the Spirit of God. The arguments have been presented. The seed has been sown, and now it will spring up and bear fruit. The publications distributed by missionary workers have exerted their influence, yet many whose minds were impressed have been prevented from fully comprehending the truth or from yielding obedience. Now the rays of light penetrate everywhere, the truth is seen in its clearness, and the honest children of God sever the bands which have held them. Family connections, church relations, are powerless to stay them now. Truth is more precious than all besides. Notwithstanding the agencies combined against the truth, a large number take their stand upon the Lord's side.[9]

Satan attempts to counterpoint the movement using similar manifestations. Ultimately, however, God the warrior appears riding on a white horse (see Revelation 19:11), and that is the end of that as far as Satan is concerned. An angel handcuffs him, drops him into a pit, pulls the cover over, and seals it. He disappears from the scene for a thousand years (see Revelation 20:1-3).

What happens during the interval?
Two things happen during the interval between the early and latter rain. First, born-again Christians advance through the process of sanctification toward what Paul calls "the prize for which God has called me heavenward in Christ Jesus" (Philippians 3:14). This process is a direct result of the baptism of the Holy Spirit that will be discussed in more detail in chapter 9. The Holy Spirit transforms (see 2 Corinthians 3:17, 18), is the effective agent in the new-birth process (see 1 Corinthians 6:11), leads minds to the truth (see 1 John 5:6), keeps the church on track and focused on her goal (see 1 Corinthians 12:7), and becomes the seal, the surety and guarantee, of our salvation (see Ephesians 1:13, 14).

The power
Besides all these good things, the Holy Spirit also works with

power. Referring back to chapter 1, you will remember that it was precisely during the interval between the early and latter rain that Jesus said the harvest was already ripe (see John 4:35). And it was precisely during this time that the gospel would advance forcefully using aggressive people (see Matthew 11:12). Nevertheless, this is the weakest point in our Adventist understanding, because, while we spend considerable time dealing with the Holy Spirit as a sanctifying agent, we spend far less time talking and learning about the power of the Holy Spirit working in our own lifetime.

Satan is alive and well on planet Earth

To understand the power of the Holy Spirit in our day, we also have to understand Satan's organizational system.

Paul is the Bible writer who outlines for us how Satan works. Luke, in the book of Acts, gives us illustrations, and Ellen White pulls it all together into a coordinated whole.

Paul talks frequently about "the powers." The key text is Ephesians 6:12:

> For our struggle is not against flesh and blood, but against rulers, against authorities, against the powers of this dark world and against the spiritual forces of evil in the heavenly realms.

These spiritual forces of evil are "world rulers" that "blind the minds of unbelievers" (2 Corinthians 4:4).

The world is in the grip of these powers. Except for the angels, who do the will of God (see Galatians 3:19), these powers are in opposition to God. A gigantic cosmic host of evil powers is holding humankind enslaved. The entire complex of the "spirit of the world" (1 Corinthians 2:12) is in this grip. These powers manifest themselves in various ways, often unseen and inexplicable. God is still ultimately in control (Romans 1:20), but the powers are nevertheless sinister influences in the world. They exercise a great deal of influence over the course of the present age.

These powers have various names:

Name	Text
Authorities	Col. 1:16
Those who govern the basic principles of this world	Gal. 4:3; Col. 2:8
Messengers of Satan	2 Cor. 12:7
Powers	Rom. 8:38; Eph. 6:12
Powers of dominion	Eph. 1:21
Demons and "rulers"	Rom. 8:38; Col. 1:16; Eph. 6:12
Spiritual forces of evil in heavenly realms	Eph. 6:12
The powers of this dark world	Eph. 6:12

In Paul's view, this whole complex of powers is a highly organized system led by Satan and administered by his evil angels. Whatever happens in the world outside of Christ is influenced by these powers.

They do not, however, have complete control. John affirms that there are good angels holding back the winds of strife until the Lord decides it is time to wind down the great controversy (see Revelation 7:1).

Disarming the powers

Paul makes the point that in spite of the complex structure the powers have in place, Jesus "disarmed the powers and authorities [and] made a public spectacle of them, triumphing over them by the cross" (Colossians 2:15). The powers fight a lost cause, but they still fight.

Facing the power of Satan

Don't underestimate the power of Satan. He is not about to give up without a fight.

It is a remarkable phenomenon that we Adventists, though we are the prime proponents of what is called "great controversy" theology, and prime advocates in our eschatology of a coming cataclysmic clash between Jesus and Satan known as the battle of Armageddon, nevertheless seem to shy away from recognizing the incredible power of the devil we see manifest all around us. Start using vocabulary like "kingdom power" and "deliverance" in an Adventist audience, and all of a sudden people kind of move over to the other side of the room, feeling that things are beginning to sound fanatical.

Please don't put this book down yet. I guarantee you we are not going to step outside biblical guidelines.

How Satan ties up humanity

To understand this issue, we must first understand how Satan ties up the human race. He does four things:

1. He blinds people's spiritual eyes (2 Corinthians 4:4).
2. He blocks spiritual discernment (1 Corinthians 2:14).
3. He causes people to see evil as good and thus negates the power of the gospel (Romans 1:24).
4. He distorts spiritual discernment with false doctrine (Revelation 14:8).

Power for effective evangelism

By power, we mean something that is active. It works. Pew potatoes do not have power. Passive, inactive Christians do not have power. People who have only an intellectual attachment to Christianity do not have power. Born-again but undiscipled Christians do not have power.[10]

The gospel is power—the power of God unto salvation (see Romans 1:16).

The power for effective evangelism, the means of undoing

what Satan has done, comes only from the Holy Spirit.

Please notice that I did not say that power for evangelism comes from the Holy Spirit. I said that power for *effective* evangelism comes from the Holy Spirit.

It is possible to do a lot of churchy things without the power of the Holy Spirit. You can even win souls without the power of the Holy Spirit. You can convince people with logic. You can inundate people with biblical data. You can even talk people to death to the point that they may join the church just to get rid of you. None of this, however, constitutes *effective* evangelism.

Effective evangelism only happens when the Holy Spirit is allowed to work in such a way that three things transpire:

1. People's minds are unchained from the power of Satan.
2. Their spiritual eyes are enlightened.
3. The power of the gospel takes effect in their lives.

No logic, power of persuasion, evangelistic technology, or power of personality can pull this off. None of these things can occur without the aid and influence of the Holy Spirit.

People's minds are unchained when the gospel is presented with power. That doesn't mean with a large amplifier and a "loud cry." It means through a dynamic personal testimony that rings true. It means saying what you say about the Lord with conviction in your voice and enthusiasm in your body language. It means beating the blahs in your own life and getting out and beating the bushes for converts, because unless you and I do it, somebody is going to miss heaven.

Is the Holy Spirit a Pentecostal? Far from it. He has left the Pentecostals far behind—along with some of us! He is way out in front. Look at it this way:

> You are getting the coming of the Lord too far off. I saw the latter rain was coming as the midnight cry [the Millerite movement], *and with ten times the power.*[11]

So, go fill up your tank, Adventist member. Let's get some power to the wheels!

1. Jan Paulsen, *When the Spirit Descends* (Washington, D.C.: Review and Herald Publishing Association, 1977), 7.

2. *Testimonies to Ministers and Gospel Workers*, 174, emphasis mine.

3. Ibid., 174, 175, emphasis mine.

4. Speaking in tongues is *the big issue* that causes so much controversy and makes noncharismatics reticent even to talk about the Holy Spirit. If you are interested in studying more, the following resources will be helpful:

John Robertson, *Tongues: What You Should Know About Glossolalia* (Boise, Idaho: Pacific Press Publishing Association, 1978).

Nicholas Fisher, *Understanding Tongues* (England: Stanborough Press Limited, n.d.).

John F. MacArthur, *Charismatic Chaos* (Grand Rapids: Zondervan Publishing House, 1992).

5. This is a one-sentence summary of a very large topic. Further discussion and study is beyond the scope of this book.

6. This passage is Mark's version of the great commission. There is some discussion as to whether Mark 16:9-20 is actually part of the Bible or not, because two early manuscripts do not contain these verses. For more information, see the *SDA Bible Commentary*, 5: 658. If you are interested in more details, look in a Bible commentary such as *The Interpreter's Bible* (Nashville: Abingdon Press, 1957), vol. 7. In any case, Ellen White uses this text as a takeoff point to describe the phenomena that will happen during the latter rain.

7. See *Early Writings*, 271.

8. *The Acts of the Apostles*, 55; *Christ's Object Lessons*, 118.

9. *The Great Controversy*, 612.

10. It seems strange there could be such a person. Look up Luke 15:25-31 to read about one of them.

11. Ellen White, *Spalding and Magan Collection* 4, emphasis mine.

CHAPTER 4

Why Bobby Allen Is Still a Catholic

My first attempt at soul winning was not very successful. Of course, I was only ten years old, so maybe you wouldn't expect too much. I had learned about the prophecies in Sabbath School class, and I decided the time had come to evangelize my friend next door. His name was Bobby Allen.

Bobby Allen was a Catholic. I knew where Catholics fit in the prophetic scheme of things, so I figured the best approach was to hit the issue head-on. We were standing by the gate that divided our two yards. I said, "Bobby, I think that deep down in his heart, the pope really knows he is wrong, don't you?" Bobby Allen's reaction to my evangelization was immediate and swift. He took a swing at me and left me lying on the lawn with a world-class bleeding nose! So much for the confrontational approach.

Some lessons are hard to learn. Years later, a friend and I were sitting on the lawn in front of the library in Reno, Nevada. We were working at a forestry camp in the mountains earning money for the next school year and had come down to Reno to spend the Sabbath. We didn't know where the church was, so we sat down on the lawn in front of the library reading our Bibles. Suddenly this man appeared out of nowhere and asked, "Are those Bibles you boys have there? I used to believe in the Bible," he said, "until I discovered that during the war [World War II], people on both sides were praying to kill people on the other side. Since these people were all Christians, I decided they were all wrong, and so was the Bible. So now I am an agnostic."

I went for the confrontational approach again. "The Bible," I remarked, "talks about people just like you. It says right here in 2 Peter 3:3 that in the last days there will come scoffers walking after their own lusts." That, of course, went over like a lead balloon.

"See," he said, "Christians hate everybody!"

The Jesus approach

Jesus took a direct approach sometimes, as in cleansing the temple, but most of the time He took a different tack, and Ellen White tells us that Jesus' way of dealing with people cannot be improved on.[1]

In this chapter, we will study how Satan has chained up the human mind and spirit; how Jesus' method of working with people unchains minds and lives; take a look at some specific experiences in Jesus' ministry; and outline some specific principles of dealing with people and presenting spiritual truth.

Is soul winning worth the effort?

First of all, we need again to emphasize the high value the Lord places on the science of soul winning. Paul brought this out when he said, "I have become all things to all men so that by all possible means I might save some. I do all this for the sake of the gospel, that I may share in its blessings" (1 Corinthians 9:22, 23). Ellen White calls soul winning "the highest of all sciences." "The greatest work to which human beings can aspire," she says, "is the work of winning men from sin to holiness."[2]

The science of soul winning

Ellen White gave us an interesting clue when she called soul winning a science, implying that there is a technique to doing it. Dealing with human minds, she wrote in 1880, is "the nicest job that was ever committed to mortal man."[3] To most of us, *nice* means enjoyable or pleasant, but it has the secondary meaning of showing discernment and subtlety, requiring great accuracy, precision, and skill.[4] That was its primary meaning in the 1800s. That's what Jesus meant when He said, "I am sending you out like sheep among wolves. Therefore be as *shrewd as snakes* and as *innocent as doves*" (Matthew 10:16). Those words imply the use of sociological and psychological principles in dealing with people.

I got called down in a seminar one Sabbath afternoon when I talked about the technology of church growth. A brother objected to applying the word *technology* to church work, because in his view it was an insult to the Holy Spirit. If the church, he felt, was spiritual enough, you wouldn't have to talk about technology. In his view, the right degree of spirituality automatically kicks in the right methodology.

The Bible, however, does not agree with this brother's viewpoint, nor does Ellen White. Consider the following statements on soul-winning methodology:

> *Solomon.* "The fruit of the righteous is a tree of life, and he who wins souls is wise" (Proverbs 11:30). The word Solomon uses for "wise" here has the connotation of a person who is skillful in doing technical work.[5]

> *Paul.* "Though I am free and belong to no man, I make myself a slave to everyone, to win as many as possible. To the Jews, I became like a Jew, to win the Jews. . . . To those not having the law I became like one not having the law, . . . so as to win those not having the law. To the weak I became weak, to win the weak. I have become all things to all men so that by all possible means I might save some" (1 Corinthians 9:19-22).

> *Ellen White*: "The study of the workers now should be to learn the *trade of gathering souls* into the gospel net" (*Review and Herald*, 8 Dec. 1885, emphasis mine).

> "It is highly important that a pastor mingle much with his people, and thus become *acquainted with the different phases of human nature*. He should *study the workings of the mind*, that he may adapt his teachings to the intellect of his hearers" (*Gospel Workers*, 191, emphasis mine).

"Mechanics, lawyers, merchants, men of all trades and professions, educate themselves that they may become masters of their business. Should the followers of Christ be less intelligent, and while professedly engaged in His service be ignorant of the ways and means to be employed? The enterprise of gaining everlasting life is above every earthly consideration. *In order to lead souls to Jesus there must be a knowledge of human nature and a study of the human mind.* Much careful thought and fervent prayer are required to know how to approach men and women upon the great subject of truth" (*Testimonies for the Church*, 4:67, emphasis mine).

How Satan chains up humankind

As we mentioned in chapter 3, Satan works with four key methods to chain up the human race:
1. He blinds people's spiritual eyes (2 Corinthians 4:4).
2. He blocks spiritual discernment (1 Corinthians 2:14).
3. He causes people to see evil as good and thus negates the power of the gospel (Romans 1:24).
4. He distorts spiritual discernment with false doctrine (Revelation 14:8).

Jesus used methods that exactly counterpoint Satan's system. By following these methods and relying on the Holy Spirit, any member can become a successful witness and soul winner.

Jesus' method outlined

Jesus did two things. First, He used basic principles of persuasion to reach people's thinking processes and their hearts. Second, He used sound principles of teaching. We'll outline His teaching principles in chapter 7. For now, let's look at His way of reaching people's thinking processes and hearts.

Ellen White gives us the basic system Jesus used:

Christ's method alone will give true success in reaching the people. The Saviour mingled with men as one who desired their good. He showed His sympathy for them, ministered to their needs, and won their confidence. Then He bade them, "Follow Me."[6]

Jesus was a people-person who made those around Him feel that He cared, with no hidden agendas. Once He gained their confidence, teaching the truth was easy.

The second part of His method is more technological. It has to do with how truth is presented. Consider the following statement:

> We must have more than an intellectual belief in the truth. . . . When truth is held as truth only by the conscience, when the heart is not stimulated and made receptive, only the mind is affected. But when the truth is received as truth by the heart, it has passed through the conscience, and has captivated the soul with its pure principles. It is placed in the heart by the Holy Spirit, who reveals its beauty to the mind, that its transforming power may be seen in the character (*Evangelism*, p. 291).

Let's look at this statement and some accompanying concepts from the same page in *Evangelism,* in the form of a chart.

A truth —	**Intellect** —	Accepted as logical and "true" Acted on as a	— **Conscience** —	**Heart**
A doctrine or some lifestyle principle	Information	piece of true information "Men may turn from one doctrine to another . . . yet they may know nothing of the meaning of the words 'A new heart also I will give you.' "	"When truth is held as truth only by the conscience, when the heart is not stimulated and made receptive, only the mind is affected."	Emotions "It is placed in the heart by the Holy Spirit, who reveals its beauty to the mind, that its transforming power may be seen in the character."

Jesus and Nicodemus's heart

The story of Jesus' dealings with Nicodemus shows how He went through the process in the chart on the previous page. First of all, let's look at who Nicodemus was. He was a high-up official in the temple hierarchy. He knew his doctrines. There was little that Jesus could say that would "inform" Nicodemus. He already had information. What he did not have was "heart." There were any number of people around claiming to be the Messiah, and maybe Nicodemus had checked out more than one. Most of the pretenders to the title were politically oriented, but it was Jesus' miracles that impressed Nicodemus, so he took a chance on sneaking in an interview under cover of darkness (see John 3:2).

Nicodemus's background and studies told him that Jesus just might be the true Messiah. That put him at the point of conscience. A conviction was telling his mind that something new and different might be coming down the nerve endings! Jesus knew what Pharisees believed and how they processed their information. He also knew that Pharisees specialized in information, not "heart."[7] At the same time, Jesus recognized that Nicodemus's conscience was telling him something.

Jesus went for the heart. He made a straight statement about the new birth. That was not an unknown concept to Nicodemus, except that for him, "birth," as a descendent of Abraham, already assured his place in the kingdom. That's why he referred only to physical birth when he questioned Jesus (see John 3:4).

Jesus' rebirth statement piqued his interest, however. Jesus gently put Nicodemus on the spot by calling into question the depth of his understanding of the Old Testament teachings on the new birth (see Jeremiah 31 and Ezekiel 11).

Then Jesus connected with John the Baptist by talking about water baptism. John was a popular figure at the time, and Nicodemus had probably studied out the water-baptism issue. Jesus used that as a takeoff point to talk about the Holy Spirit and get to the core of the issue. He took Nicodemus back to the Old Testament, familiar ground again, and made a new application of a familiar story—the snake on the cross in the desert. From there, He nailed down what Nicodemus came to find out. Only the real Messiah has direct communication with heaven;

that's why Jesus could do miracles.

Now He hits Nicodemus for a decision. "This is the verdict," Jesus said. "You love darkness, or you love light. Your deeds fit with darkness. You want the kingdom, you come into the light" (John 3:19-21, paraphrased).

Four principles

Jesus used four principles in this encounter.

1. Be aware of the person's background. Talk to him, not to your own theories.
2. Speak directly to the heart and its needs.
3. Don't argue. Jesus bypassed possible arguments over details and kept to the point.
4. Present the cross and its results—a gospel presentation.

Did it work?

What happened to Nicodemus? We know that he became an undercover follower (see John 7:50-52). We also know he went public at the time of the crucifixion (John 19:39, 40). Ellen White tells us that he became the mainstay of the early church:

> Now, when the disciples were scattered and discouraged, Nicodemus came boldly to the front. He was rich, and he employed his wealth to sustain the infant church of Christ, that the Jews thought would be blotted out with the death of Jesus. He who had been so cautious and questioning, now, in the time of peril, was firm as the granite rock, encouraging the flagging faith of the followers of Christ, and furnishing means to carry on the cause. He was defrauded, persecuted, and stigmatized by those who had paid him reverence in other days. He became poor in this world's goods, yet he faltered not in the faith that had its beginning in that secret night conference with the young Galilean.[8]

John 4—the woman at Jacob's well

The second incident that demonstrates the principles Jesus used is recorded in John 4. (The following analysis will be more helpful if you read the story first).

This was a different situation than the Nicodemus encounter. This woman was not an Israelite, though she had a theological/nationalistic ax to grind. She had some major personal problems that Jesus helped her solve, as well as straightening out her theology.

Jesus again went to the core of the issue. He used His prophetic gift, which you and I probably don't have, but He also utilized tools that anyone can learn to use. Basically, Jesus did six things:

1. He got her attention.
2. He piqued her interest.
3. He motivated a desire on her part.
4. He moved her toward conviction.
5. He intensified her desire and conviction.
6. He got a decision and action from her.

Notice how He did it.

His first statement aroused her interest. Verse 9 explains why— Jews do not associate with Samaritans.	(1) "Will you give me a drink?"
His second statement piqued her interest.	(2) "If you knew the gift of God and who it is that asks you for a drink, you would ask him and he would give you living water."
His third statement stimulated her desire.	(3) "Everyone who drinks this water will thirst again, but whoever drinks the water I give will never thirst again."

His fourth and fifth statements implanted conviction.	(4) "Go, call your husband." (This is the gift of prophecy at work.) (5) "You are right to say you have no husband— you have had five, and are now living with a man."
His sixth and seventh statements intensified desire and conviction.	(6) "The time is coming . . . true worshipers will worship the Father in spirit and in truth." (7) "I who speak to you am he." *Jesus was never this direct with His own people.*
He got action	"Come see a man who told me everything I ever did!" The people run out to see Jesus.

In even more detail, notice the different kinds of desire that popped up in this woman during this conversation. The point is that Jesus used normal human emotions and desires to lead her down the road to conviction and decision.

"Give me a drink"	Desire for approval, the im- plication of social approval, coming from a Jewish male.
"If you knew"	Desire to know—no one wants to be ignorant.
God has a gift for you	Desire to acquire—curiosity.
"Who it is who speaks to you"	Desire for identity.

"Give you living water"	Desire for something better.
"Whoever drinks . . . will never thirst again"	Desire for permanent satisfaction.
"The water I give . . ."	Desire to get something free.
"A spring of water . . . eternal life"	Desire for a more abundant life.
"Spring of water welling up"	Desire for something beneficial.
"Eternal life"	Desire for self-preservation.
"You have well said . . ."	Desire for reputation.
"Worship what you do not know"	Desire for identity.
"True worshipers"	Desire for self-worth.
"The kind of worshipers the Father seeks"	Desire to know God and to make one's life what it ought to be.

Everyone responds to this method

The Gospels tell about all kinds of people who responded to Jesus' methods. Mary Magdalene, a well-known prostitute, became so attached to Jesus that she broke all social conventions by sneaking into a banquet and bathing His feet with perfume and pouring some on His head (see Matthew 26:6-13; Luke 7:18-35). We don't do this kind of thing, so it is hard for us to grasp just how much significance it had for Mary. We tend to think how much the perfume cost (the same problem Judas had). Simon, the host, only thought in terms of who Mary was (he seemed to know a lot about her as a prostitute!). Mary was just so overwhelmingly happy with what Jesus had done for her that she *had* to express herself. She did it the best way she knew how.

Jesus worked with Pharisees, tax collectors, rich people, an adulteress, fishermen, all kinds of people. His methods worked, and they became the nucleus of a new world order—the Christian church.

Soul winning is a science that all Christians are expected to know about and learn how to do. It is a normal part of discipleship. The way the truth is presented often has much to do in determining whether it will be accepted or rejected. The approach I used with Bobby Allen didn't work. I have since learned that Jesus has a better way.

In the next chapter, we will study an approach modeled after Jesus' method that you and your church family can use on a regular basis to talk to your friends, neighbors, and acquaintances about the gospel and the Adventist message.

1. *Evangelism*, 56.
2. *The Ministry of Healing*, 398.
3. *Evangelism*, 348.
4. *Webster's II: New Riverside Dictionary*, s.v. "nice."
5. R. Laird Harris, *Theological Wordbook of the Old Testament* (Chicago: Moody Press, 1980), 1:284.
6. *The Ministry of Healing*, 143. For a book-length explanation of how this system works, see Philip G. Samaan, *Christ's Way of Reaching People* (Hagerstown, Md.: Review and Herald Publishing Association, 1990).
7. Specializing in information at the expense of "heart " does not mean a person is irreligious. You can read about some very good Pharisees in George Knight, *The Pharisee's Guide to Perfect Holiness* (Boise, Idaho: Pacific Press, 1992).
8. *The Spirit of Prophecy*, 2:135, 136.

CHAPTER 5

The Friendship Factor

A friend of mine walked out of a meeting with a group of civic leaders in an inner-city neighborhood and came face to face with a man asking for a handout. My friend was mad about something that had happened in the meeting, and his reaction was fast and curt. He grabbed a few dollar bills from his pocket, threw them down on the sidewalk, yelled, "Here, take it!" and walked away.

The man hollered after him, "Hey, come back here and pick it up. I don't need your money that bad!"

It was an embarrassing moment.

"Hey, man," he said, "I may be poor, but I still got some dignity."

My friend, to his everlasting credit, went back and apologized profusely.

"What if that guy shows up in church some Sabbath and discovers I'm the pastor?" he asked later. "What kind of a witness was that for the gospel?"

Friendship evangelism

This brings us to the subject of this chapter—friendship evangelism.

Friendship evangelism means that wherever you are, whatever you are doing, you consciously work at building relationships that will open doors to lead people to the gospel. It also means that a process is developed by your church, and you as a person, that *creates relationships with people* prior to their commitment to the Lord or their decision to be baptized and join the church.

Simply put, what you *do* shouts a lot louder than what you say!

First impressions

There are times when relationship building is so critical that bungling the job can short-circuit a person's entry into the church.

Consider this: A church member had been working for ten years with a friend of hers, and the Sabbath arrived when the woman finally decided to attend church. They drove into the parking lot, and as they got out of the car, a greeter met them. Recognizing the member, but not the guest, the greeter said, "You must be visiting our church today."

"Yes," the woman answered.

The greeter replied, "I thought you were a visitor, because *you don't look like us!*"

I leave it to you to figure out what happened next! Ten years of work gone in seconds! Five misspoken words was all it took!

This experience points out a vital principle of soul winning— *lasting impressions are made in the first thirty seconds, and within five minutes people decide whether they will come back to your church or not.*

When nonattender Herman Ciniscouchi walks into church one Sabbath morning for the first time in three years, and a greeter says "Hey, Herman, it's about time you came back to church," can you really blame him if he walks right back out and doesn't come back for another three years, or until that greeter dies, whichever comes first?

Evangelism that produces dropouts

The process by which people come into the church has a great deal to do with whether they stick.

Sociological research shows that some ways of doing evangelism and winning souls actually produce more dropouts than stay-ins.

1. *A manipulative approach.* A manipulative approach to evangelism is hard to define, but easy to "feel."

The feeling of being manipulated is a perception that forms in a person's mind. It doesn't have much to do with the content of the message being communicated. It's the body language and personality of the person doing the evangelizing that produces an "I'm being taken" feeling.

Let us clearly understand what we mean. "Manipulative" does *not* mean that the person doing the evangelization is dishonest. It means that the *way* he or she goes about it somehow gives the message itself a phony ring.

It is kind of like watching a carpenter try to pound nails with the claw end of the hammer and pull nails with the head. You wouldn't have much confidence in such a person.

The logic of a presentation may be flawless and may well convince a person, even against his or her will. Sometimes a presentation does an incomplete job of convincing, though on the surface a person may say Yes. But the sticking power is not there.

There are three common manipulative approaches.

Telling, but not listening. Pouring out information about spiritual facts, or a Bible doctrine, is a common way of doing evangelism. It is assumed that correct understanding of the facts will result in a decision.

The problem is that the fact giving is too often a one-way communication. One person talks, and the other person listens but does not actively participate in the learning process. Research shows that 75 percent of people say No when approached this way with the gospel.

It is difficult for us to realize that this is a manipulative approach, because it is precisely what we do most of the time. It does not seem manipulative to us on the giving end. But it is often *perceived* as manipulative by people on the receiving end, unless a relationship is established at the same time information is pouring out. The facts, by themselves, seldom get through permanently.

Notice again that Jesus built relationships before He asked for a commitment:

The Savior mingled with men as one who desired their good. He showed His sympathy for them, ministered to their needs, and *won their confidence. Then* He bade them, 'Follow me.'[1]

Manipulative dialogue. This is a kind of "close the sale" approach. It centers on an overly emotional appeal or a set of memorized questions.

A good example is what you get when Jehovah's Witnesses knock on your door. It is a "canned message," memorized and regurgitated.

Another example is the long, drawn-out appeal sometimes used at public evangelistic meetings. Someone out there says in his mind, "You know, if I don't go forward and get this over with, I'm going to miss my bus!" This kind of thinking seldom shows on the surface, but underneath it goes on all the time.

Manipulative dialogue is momentarily effective, but often not permanent. Research shows that 81 percent of people approached this way say Yes. Of that group, however, 85 percent become inactive within a year. On a graph, it looks like this:

Say Yes

Still active a year later

Nonmanipulative dialogue. Two-way interaction is the way to go. This is what Paul was talking about when he wrote:

You yourselves are our letter, written on our hearts, known and read by everybody. You show that you are a letter from Christ, the result of our ministry, written not with ink but with the spirit of the living God, not on tablets of stone but on tablets of human hearts (2 Corinthians 3:2, 3).

Nonmanipulative dialogue is what makes small groups so effective. Information is still poured out, but in a setting that allows people to ask questions, react to what is being presented, and become part of the process through which truth is learned and assimilated. At the same time, relationships are established, and truth becomes "living."

Using this approach, 99 percent say Yes, and of those, 96 percent stick.

Say Yes

Stay

2. *An evangelization process that seeks only decisions* rather than making disciples.

The reason this approach produces dropouts is that it is assumed that once a person goes through a baptismal ceremony, he or she is automatically assimilated into the congregation, a kind of "dunk 'em and drop 'em" philosophy.

Discipleship, on the other hand, is an ongoing process that assimilates people into the life of the church by intention and design over a period of time. Unfortunately, most Adventist churches have no organized, intentional assimilation system in place. Whatever happens, happens by accident. That is one of the main reasons we have to have periodic reclamation projects to ferret out nonattendees and ex-Adventists.

3. *One-time presentation.* An evangelization process that presents the gospel one time and immediately asks for a response tends to create dropouts.

Research shows that the most active members of a church are exposed to church life 5.79 times before they make a commitment. They make some friends, attend church social events, and move in and around the church before making a commitment. The more exposure they have to the church and its family before they make a commitment, the more likely they are to stay in the church afterward.

It's whom you know!

So what it comes down to is that it's not so much *what* you know as it is *whom* you know!

Summing up, it is not the quality of the information we pass on to people in the form of sermons, Bible studies, evangelistic presentations, Revelation seminars, et al. that makes the most difference. Rather, it is the *quality of the relationships built up* while the information is being given that makes the difference.

Five major stages

This is clearly demonstrated by the fact that people usually go through five stages in the process of coming into the church.

Stage One: Awareness. They discover that the church exists and learn what it stands for. This stage is often initiated through media ministry, Adventist books and magazines, or community service programs.

Stage Two: Interest. Something triggers their interest in a particular local church. Often the Holy Spirit makes them receptive and motivates them to go looking for a certain church.

Stage Three: Evaluation. They go to a meeting, a Bible study, or some other function of the church, to kind of "check it out."

This is the really critical point. When they first arrive, the first thirty seconds are vital, and within five minutes they have formed a perception. This is why a church needs to develop a well-trained receptionist ministry.

Stage Four: Tryout. They come back again and again. They are consciously or unconsciously trying the church on for size. This period may last from three months to two years.

The Catholics have a theory about a place called limbo, where unbaptized children go if they die while someone decides what to do with them. We don't believe such a thing, of course, but we do tend to create, however unintentionally, a sort of sociological "Limboland" in our churches for nonbaptized people.

If you think about it, in the Adventist psyche people are not really "in" until they are baptized. What happens between the time they first begin visiting church and their baptism? Are they visitors? Not really, because they may be there regularly. Are they guests? Yes and no. Are they members? No, but then again, sort of! Are they "friends of the church"? Well, yes and no, again. So what are they?

This is where friendship evangelism comes into play. Making people feel like part of the family, even before formal ceremonial admission, is critically important.

Stage Five: Adoption. This is the point where the person becomes part of the social fabric of the church.

Research shows that if people make *six new friends* during the first year of membership, they will probably stay. If not, they will probably drop out. An ongoing small-group ministry is vital in the life of the church for this very reason. Joining a small group almost automatically produces a network of friends.

What did you say?

We said earlier that what you *do* shouts a lot louder than what you say! *How you listen* also makes a much greater impact than what you say. This is a key component of friendship evangelism.

My daughter has been after me for some time to go and get a hearing test. She claims, along with some other members of the family, that I may need a hearing aid pretty soon. She came home the other day with an interesting comment, however. A hearing specialist friend of hers whom she talked to about me said that I probably was just suffering from a typical husband-father malady called "selective listening." Right on! (I'm working on this, by the way. Husbands/fathers, take note!).

There is a lesson in this. You and I hear what we want to hear, but what we *want* to hear is usually not what we *ought* to hear. Friendship evangelism means that we will all teach ourselves the art of listening for what we *ought* to hear.

A mini course on how to listen

You are about to take a mini course on how to listen. Follow carefully.

Hearing people's story

Everyone has a "story." Somewhere deep down inside of our minds is the real story that makes us tick. It is made up of memories, experiences, and perceptions. It keeps popping out.

If you learn how to listen, you can "hear" that story, and if it is a hindrance to spiritual growth, you can help a person rebuild it so that it is a help to spiritual growth.

How to "hear" the story

A person's story is usually not expressed in words. It is expressed in feelings, body language, and actions. You get at a person's story by learning to do three things:

1. Observe. Most of us are so interested in ourselves and our own story that we don't even see, much less hear, other people.

The first step is to observe people's body language and to listen carefully for emotionally loaded words.

Let me illustrate. Some time ago we visited a church, and a particular member caught our eye. This woman was sitting where she could see the entrance door, and it was obvious from her body language that she was giving every person who entered the once-over to see if they measured up to some image she had in mind. It was amusing to watch. We started calculating between ourselves who measured up to her mental image and who did not. As you can guess, the positive count was very, very low!

Her actions said very loudly that there was a story hidden in there someplace, and it was not a positive one. Whatever it was, it was eating her up and twisting her around to become the judge and jury of the rest of the church membership.

Later, I learned this woman's story. She had suffered most of her life because of erroneous advice received years before from church leaders who should have known better. Because of her own twisted experience and what was done in the name of the Lord, she was deeply hurt and unhappy and certainly did not want anyone else to be happy. Hence her obviously judgmental and mean spirit. This poor soul was trying to atone for something that was not hers to atone for. What a sad story.

Ask the right questions. How and under what circumstances you ask a question will either open or close mental doors. The very same question can come across as either manipulative and confrontational or nonmanipulative and nonconfrontational.

It is the nonmanipulative and nonconfrontational questions that open mental doors. Unfortunately, human nature makes many commonplace questions come out sounding confrontational.

For instance, a simple, apparently innocent question like "What did you do today?" asked of someone you do not know well can be very threatening. In some heads it invokes answers like, "What business is it of yours?" or "I wonder if this person saw me . . . ?"

On the other hand, a question like "Would you explain that to me?" asked during a conversation is less threatening because you are simply asking for clarification. Depending on the circumstances, the answer may well incorporate bits and pieces of their "story." Astute listening will begin to piece it together.

Feeling check. "Feeling check" might sound like some mind-probe technique out of "Star Trek," but it's not. It is just a simple way of getting a person's story.

Most of us like to think that we run and operate on logic and "thinking." That's not true. Most of us run on emotions and feelings. *A feeling check is an observation with a follow-up question.* The observation/question must include the name of an emotion. For example, you might say, "Somehow I have the impression that you are discouraged today. Did I get that right?" Or, "I would guess that you might be feeling offended by what went on in the boss's office this morning. Is that correct?"

Notice that in each case an emotion is mentioned. The first is "discouraged"; the second is "feeling offended." Then a follow-up question allows the person to respond to the question in his/her own way. Feeling-check expressions start with phrases like, "I am guessing that . . . ," "Somehow I get the impression that . . . ," It appears as if . . ."

Attend a Friendship Evangelism seminar

We can't go into more depth in this short chapter, but you can attend, or study on your own, a Friendship Evangelism seminar.

The materials are available from Concerned Communications, Highway 59 North, Siloam Springs, AR 72761. This course, written by Monte Sahlin, adult ministries coordinator of the North American Division Church Ministries Department, will open your eyes and train you in how to use friendship evangelism effectively in your life and in your church.

Consider this statement carefully:

If we would humble ourselves before God, and *be kind and courteous and tenderhearted and pitiful, there would be one hundred conversions to the truth where now there is only one.* But, though professing to be converted, we carry around with us a bundle of self that we regard as altogether too precious to be given up. It is our privilege to lay this burden at the feet of Christ and in its place take the character and similitude of Christ. The Savior is waiting for us to do this.[2]

Friendship evangelism! You can do it. Your family can do it. Your church can do it. So let's go do it!

---

1. *The Ministry of Healing*, 143.
2. *Testimonies for the Church*, 9:189, emphasis mine.

CHAPTER 6

The Indispensable Man

It happened on an island in the Caribbean. I was studying with a man who came to my church regularly. I went to his house every week for a Bible study, and I was sure he would make a decision for baptism and church membership soon. He was really interested! I even had the deacons primed for his upcoming baptism.

And then it happened. One night we studied about health reform and clean and unclean meat. As soon as we finished the study, he said, "If this is true, what am I going to do with the pig out in the shed that I'm fattening up for Christmas?" I had seen that pig, and it was b-i-g!

"Well," I said, "you could sell it or give it away or just let it go."

"Oh, no," he answered, "I have too much invested to do any of those things. This is a very special pig!"

A lot of tender loving care had gone into that Christmas pig. It was the man's prized possession, and his family members were anxiously awaiting Christmas because of that pig.

We were at a crisis point.

"What do I do?" he asked again.

"Well," I said, "I guess you have to choose between Jesus and the pig."

There was a long silence. Finally it came out.

"I guess I'll go for the pig."

That was the end of the studies. He never came back to church. He wanted no more contact with us at all.

He listened to a voice and made a choice. Not the right one, unfortunately.

So many voices

There are hundreds of voices out there calling. People are bombarded with TV, magazines, videos, books—you name it.

There are a multitude of religious voices out there. New Agers talk about their out-of-body experiences, Jehovah's Witnesses talk about their coming kingdom, Mormons talk about family values, fundamentalists talk about the inroads of secularism and the lack of prayer in schools, evangelicals talk about the cross, and Pentecostals talk in tongues no one understands, while Hollywood and the entertainment industry take every opportunity to put down Christianity and promote secularism and materialism.[1]

Who to believe?

So many choices

I once lived in a country where you had no choice. Every citizen was automatically a member of the popular church. It was constitutionally mandated. If you wanted to get married through a civil ceremony instead of in the cathedral, you had to be officially excommunicated from a church you never belonged to by choice.

When Martin Luther started the Protestant Reformation, he gave people two choices: "Protestant" or Roman Catholic. There is something dynamic about protesting, so a lot of people opted to abandon the Catholics and go with Luther, Calvin, and other reformers.

But it was still not really a free choice. The Europeans invented a territorial system where an area was either Protestant or Catholic according to the religion of the *ruler*, not the people. It was called the "territorial church." You could change your religion just by moving across the street!

But today, because there are so many voices, there are also a lot of choices.[2] Believe it or not, the fastest-growing religious community in North America turns out to be Islam, not even a Christian religion! One of the fastest-growing churches in the Los Angeles area, for instance, is a Buddhist temple.

So many roads to travel

Things are a lot different today. You can travel any road you want. Baby boomers who dropped out of religion altogether are starting to come back because they realize their children need some moral values. But they are picky about the kind of church they will come back to. They return to a church whose liturgy and ways of doing things lack dynamics, participation, and are basically boring and unresponsive to human needs.

Buddhists are not all Orientals, and Hindus are not all from India. So-called Anglo churches are a mixture of everybody, and Black Muslims, or the Nation of Islam, are gaining converts at an ever-increasing rate because they are actively involved in meeting human needs in the inner cities of North America.

In this day and age, everyone goes everywhere, and some people go nowhere!

In all this pluralism and religious jumble, are there any handles to hang on to?

Who needs religion?

The fact of the matter is that in the midst of all the various voices, choices, and roads, a lot of people are looking for a religious experience. There has never been a society in the history of humankind that did not seek some kind of religion.[3] Even hard-core secular scientists are looking in new directions for a religious experience.[4]

On the following page, the first diagram shows where religion fits into human society.

Religion is the element of society that gives us understanding of the universe in which we live and assurance that life has meaning. The human psyche demands these handles, and people consciously or unconsciously search for them.

What the voices believe

Each voice out there has a set of beliefs, divided into four common denominators: founders, gods, scriptures, and way of salvation. The second diagram on the next page shows what six major world religions believe about these four categories:

Elements of society	Economics	Social	Political	Religion	Aesthetic	Legal
What it does	Use and application of **resources**	Use and application of **relationships**	Use and application of **power**	Use and application of systems of **explanation and meaning**	Use and application of **beauty**	Use and application of **legitimacy**
Family		Primary application				
Market	Primary application					
Government			Primary application			
Church	Applicable to all elements of society					

	Paganism	Hinduism	Buddhism	Islam	Judaism	Secularism
Founder	Ancestors	None	Buddha	Mohammed	Abraham	Various
God(s)	Many	Infinite number	None	One—Allah	One—Yahweh	None
Scriptures	Legends and myths	Sacred books	Writings	Koran	Old Testament plus traditions	Philosophy
Way of salvation	Appease gods and spirits	Good works	Self denial	Obedience	Good works—ethics	None needed

Focus on founders

The difference between all these religions and Christianity is that (1) their founders are all dead, and (2) believers have to work their own way to heaven, if they believe in one.

Christianity is different because its adherents follow a living founder, resurrected by the power He carried within Himself, who is "the same yesterday and today and forever" (Hebrews 13:8).[5] Resurrection power is what drove the missionary enterprise of the early church, and the promise of another resurrection at the second coming is what drives the Christian church today (see Acts 17:30, 31; 1 Thessalonians 4:13-18).

Choices demand decisions

All religions demand a decision from their followers. A Hindu has to make a decision as to whether his lifestyle will bring him back, through reincarnation, to a better social standing or as a mosquito. A Buddhist has to make a decision on how long to chant each day to get closer to a higher plane of being. A Muslim has to make a decision whether to let fate take its course or to defy it and hope for the best. An animist has to make a decision whether his or her actions will appease or irritate the gods and spirits. Even a secularist has to make a decision about the effects the decision itself will produce.

Christians, however, make a different kind of decision. We make a decision to accept a redemptive sacrifice made by a God-man named Jesus of Nazareth. We call Him Jesus (His name) Christ (His title)—Jesus the anointed one. When we call Him that, we are making a confession. We are confessing that we believe this man, Jesus, born in Nazareth in Palestine about 4 B.C., is the Messiah, the promised Redeemer, the Saviour of the world. All that is contained in the name and title we use.

The indispensable man

The Christian church started its ministry preaching in the temple and from house to house that "Jesus is *the* Christ" (Acts 5:42), but it wasn't long before the name and the title became one (see Matthew 1:1). James, probably the Lord's own brother, calls Him "*Lord* Jesus Christ," adding yet a deeper confessional dimension. Not only is He the Messiah, but James has accepted Him as his personal master or ruler.

Our religion affirms that Jesus is the key to salvation. Without accepting Him as a personal Saviour, no one gets to heaven:

> Salvation is found in no one else, for there is no other name under heaven given to men by which we must be saved (Acts 4:12).

John affirms that He was the true light that gives light to every person (John 1:9).[6] He is the indispensable man. Without Him, life eventually just stops.

A Short Bible Study on Jesus as the Indispensable Man

Introduction:

In 399 B.C. a man stood before his accusers and said, "I must obey God rather than man." That is a good statement, but the man who said it was not so good. He was bisexual, didn't work, drank a little, and was devoted to what he called "the good life." His wife thought he was just plain lazy, but some other people liked some of his teachings, so they supported him financially. The god he obeyed was, he said, a spirit that lived inside him called "diamonion." Sound familiar?

One historian says about him:

> All in all he was fortunate: he lived without working, read without writing, taught without routine, drank without dizziness, and died before senility, almost without pain.[7]

He also committed suicide, because he fell out of favor when he seduced one of the homosexual lovers of a city father.

His name was Socrates, known as the one of the greatest of the Greek philosophers, and still a hero in the intellectual world.

This man was great in the eyes of many, but he is a long way from being indispensable.

I. History Revolves Around Great People

A. **Babylon.** If you happen to know about the hanging gardens of Babylon, one of the seven wonders of the ancient world, then the name *Nebuchadnezzar* may mean something to you, but it's hardly a household word.

B. **Alexander the Great.** If you are a student of military history, Alexander will intrigue you, but he is hardly indispensable.

C. **Julius Caesar** may be better known today through movies like Cleopatra than for what he really accomplished. Actually, he is best known for being killed by his best friend, Brutus. He is still far from being indispensable.

II. Only Jesus Is Indispensable

A. **Only Jesus appears every day on our calendar, since we date everything as either "before Christ" (B.C.) or "the year of our Lord" (A.D. in Latin).**

III. What the Bible Says About Jesus

A. **Ten Great Bible Facts About Jesus**

1. He is equal with God (John 10:30).
2. He is eternal (John 1:1, 2).
3. He cooperated with the Father in the creation of this world (John 1:3).
4. He appeared as a human, as one of us (John 1:14).
5. He lived a sinless life (Hebrews 4:15).
6. He bore our sins on the cross (Romans 5:8).
7. He arose from the dead (Matthew 28:1-6).
8. He ascended to heaven as our high priest (Hebrews 8:1).
9. He is coming back again (Acts 1:9-11).
10. He will take us to the new earth (Revelation 21).

B. **What People Have Said About Jesus**

1. **John the Baptist**, His cousin: "Look, the Lamb of God, who takes away the sin of the world!" (John 1:29).
2. **Nathanael**, an early disciple: "You are the Son of God" (John 1:49).
3. **Citizens of Samaria**: "We have heard for ourselves, and we know that this man is really the Savior of the world" (John 4:42).

4. **Temple militiamen:** "No one ever spoke the way this man does" (John 7:46).

Conclusion: The Big Question: Is Jesus indispensable to you?

The Big Question for you and your family

For many years a large lump of rock lay in a shallow stream in North Carolina. People passing by saw only a typical river rock. One day a man saw it and thought it would make a good doorstop, so he took it home.

A geologist happened to pass by his house, took one look at the rock, and knew he had discovered the largest gold nugget ever unearthed east of the Rocky Mountains.

Jesus is that gold nugget for you and me. He is the indispensable man. Without Him, there is no Christian church. Without Him, there is no advent message. Without Him, there is no salvation.

What a choice!

Let's go back to my friend with the pig. He made a conscious decision to choose "the things of this world" over eternal life. Too bad, because, while he might have enjoyed that pig for one Christmas fiesta, he is going to miss the greatest fiesta of all history:

Then a voice came from the throne, saying: "Praise our God, all you his servants, you who fear him, both small and great!"

Then I heard what sounded like a great multitude, like the roar of rushing waters and like loud peals of thunder, shouting: "Hallelujah! For our Lord God Almighty reigns. Let us rejoice and be glad and give him glory! For the wedding of the Lamb has come, and his bride has made herself ready. Fine linen, bright and clean was given her to wear." . . .

Then the angel said to me, "Write: 'Blessed are those who are invited to the wedding supper of the Lamb!' " And he added, "These are the true words of God."

I saw heaven standing open and there before me was a white horse, whose rider is called Faithful and True. With justice he judges and makes war. His eyes are like blazing fire, and on his head are many crowns. He has a name written on him that no one but he himself knows. He is dressed in a robe dipped in blood, and his name is the Word of God. The armies of heaven were following him, riding on white horses and dressed in fine linen, white and clean. Out of his mouth comes a sharp sword with which to strike down the nations. "He will rule them with an iron scepter." He treads the winepress of the fury of the wrath of God Almighty. On his robe and on his thigh he has this name written: KING OF KINGS AND LORD OF LORDS (Revelation 19:5-9; 11-16).

That's Him! It's the same Jesus. Now we know why He is indispensable.

So how about you and your family, and all those people you plan to win in Jesus' name? Make the right decision now, and you'll be there.

---

1. For a survey of some of the most popular voices today, see Josh McDowell and Don Stewart, *Handbook of Today's Religions* (San Bernardino, Calif.: Here's Life Publishers, Inc., 1983), and Daniel R. Reid, ed., *Dictionary of Christianity in America* (Downers Grove, Ill.: InterVarsity Press, 1990).

2. For a survey of what North Americans believe today, see George Barna, *What Americans Believe* (Ventura, Calif.: Regal Books, 1991).

3. The downfall of the Communist empire is a case in point. Behind it all was the desire to reestablish a religious state. For some fascinating reading, see Malachi Martin, *The Keys of This Blood* (New York: Simon and Schuster, 1990).

4. See Paul Davies, *God and the New Physics* (New York: Simon and Schuster, 1984).

5. See *The Desire of Ages*, 785.

6. If you can find a copy, see R. Ruben Widmer, *Jesus, the Light of the World* (Nashville: Southern Publishing Association, 1967), for a good study of Jesus as the only means of salvation for the whole human race.

7. Will Durant, *The Story of Civilization* (New York: Simon and Schuster, 1966), 2:366.

CHAPTER 7

Teaching Teachers to Teach

When we think about evangelism, or "going to church," we usually think about preaching. Preaching is a declaratory way of presenting a message. That is to say, the preacher is the center of attention. He or she alternately explains, illustrates, or expounds on a topic or a selection of Scripture. Preaching is also exhortation. The preacher admonishes (tells, pleads with, demands of) the preachees—those who listen—with the intent that some designated action will happen.

Down through the years, preachers have themselves been exhorted to be pastor-evangelists, expository preachers, biographical preachers, inductive preachers, topical preachers, and to use creative imagination in preaching.[1] In fact, the average church pastor will preach more than two thousand sermons over a lifetime. Preaching is a great enterprise, and when done, ought to be done well.

Most of us teach

The average church member, however, will do far more teaching than preaching. Bible studies, Sabbath School lessons, discussion groups, casual conversations around the dinner table, and impromptu discussions at work are all *teaching* situations. In spite of those two thousand sermons, *religious knowledge is passed on mostly through teaching.*

Ellen White makes two unique statements about this issue. We are going to look at the statements, a question Ellen White's son asked her about the statements, and then her answer. This will give us some insights into why teaching is so vitally important. Here are the two statements:

(1) There should be less preaching, and more teaching. There are those who want more definite light than they receive from hearing the sermons. Some need a longer time than do others to understand the points presented. If the truth presented could be made a little plainer, they would see it and take hold of it, and it would be like a nail fastened in a sure place.[2]

(2) It is not preaching alone that must be done. Far less preaching is needed. More time should be devoted to patiently educating others, giving the hearers opportunity to express themselves. It is instruction that many need, line upon line, precept upon precept, here a little, and there a little.[3]

William White's question to his mother:

I have heard you say, mother, that we should have more teaching and less preaching, less preaching and more teaching,—speaking of the matter of getting the people together and having Bible readings.[4]

Ellen White's answer:

There should be less preaching and more teaching. . . .
As we approach nearer the end, I have seen that in these [camp meetings] there will be less preaching and more Bible study. There will be *little groups all over the ground with their Bibles in their hands*, and different ones leading out in a free, conversational study of the Scriptures. . . .
It has been shown me that our camp meetings are to increase in interest and success. . . .
There are those who want more definite light than they receive from hearing the sermons. Some need a longer time

than do others to understand the points presented. If truth presented could be made a little plainer, they would see it and take hold of it, and it would be like a nail fastened in a sure place (*Testimonies for the Church*, 6:87, emphasis mine).

This is a call to use small-group strategy and shift into a teaching mode.

Jesus, the Great Teacher

Jesus spent most of His time teaching. Of the ninety times He is addressed directly in the Gospels, He is called "rabbi" sixty times. That's the Greek equivalent of the Aramaic (Jesus' native language) word for "sir," but it is mostly used in the sense of "my teacher."[5] Of the remaining thirty times He is addressed, it is most commonly as a *didaskolos*, the Greek word meaning "teacher."

Jesus, the Gospels tell us, went about teaching in synagogues (see Matthew 9:35) and from village to village (see Mark 6:6), acknowledged the title of teacher (see John 13:13), and "as was his custom" spent His time teaching (Mark 10:1).

He was good at it too! The temple militiamen sent to arrest Him came back empty-handed, but with their minds filled. "No one ever spoke the way this man does" (John 7:46) was all they had to say. Talk about an impression made by good teaching!

In this chapter, we are going to take a look at some of Jesus' teaching methods. First, however, let's describe what a teaching method is.

A method is how you go about it

A teaching method is the way you present the lesson or Bible study. Every teacher uses a method, whether he or she realizes it or not. When you stand in front of your class and do all the talking, that is the lecture method. When you give a Bible study and go around the circle and have different people read Bible verses, that is a form of the discussion method.

Circumstances dictate the best method to use. For instance, if your class knows little or nothing about the subject of the lesson, you have to spend some time giving them information. You can't use the discussion method if they have nothing to discuss. On the other hand, if the lesson of the day deals with familiar territory, and your teaching goal is to make everyday-life applications, you need to use a life-application approach to the lesson.

Teaching is an art

Nevertheless, in spite of all the technology a teacher may have, in the final analysis, teaching is an art. It is a high calling from the Lord and a specific spiritual gift. The teacher's greatest reward is not getting through the lesson. It is when a student says, "Oh! Now I see!"

The principle of apperception

The first principle of teaching is known as the principle of apperception. This means that *you go from the known to the unknown.*

People, whether adults or children, are only familiar with what they know. The teacher has to move into new territory, new ideas or concepts, through the pathways of people's most familiar associations.

Let's illustrate what we are saying here from the experience of some cradle roll children. The leader has them learn the song "The consecrated cross I'll bear," but it comes out "the consecrated cross-eyed bear!" The children can relate to a cross-eyed bear; they've probably seen one in a cartoon on TV. "Cross I bear" is unknown language. The teacher's job is to move them to an understanding of what cross bearing means. That's apperception!

Theodore Roosevelt reports that he was actually afraid to go to church because he heard someone say, "The zeal of thy house has *eaten me up.*" That was a perfectly understandable phrase to David in his culture and in his native Hebrew language (see Psalm 69:9), but it was scary to a young boy in North America.

Notice on the following chart how Jesus used the principle of apperception in His teaching:

Occasion	Known	Unknown
Woman at Jacob's well (John 4)	Water	Living water
People seeking a sign (Matthew 16:1-4)	The signs of the weather	Spiritual signs of the times
Jesus' mother and brothers (Matthew 12:46-50)	Jesus' mother and brothers requested to speak to Him	Jesus explains who His spiritual mother and brothers are
Theological questions about ceremonial fasting	Using worn-out wineskins and pieces of cloth	You can't put new teachings inside old traditions

The principle of adaptation

The principle of adaptation says that the *lesson should be adapted to the individual.* This principle is really just common sense, but it takes some thought and preparation. People can't relate to what they don't know or understand, so when your teaching is put into words and illustrations they can link up with, the teaching becomes concrete and "real."

For instance, consider the story of Joseph and his brothers. Just telling the story of Joseph will have little effect. Let us say, however, that you pass out pieces of paper, ask class members to write down which part of the story is most meaningful to them, and then, if they wish, explain why. Now the class is participating. The truth of the Bible narrative is becoming real. It is being translated—adapted—to real life.

For instance, which part of the story will be especially relevant to:

1. A brother and sister who are always fighting at home?
2. The couple whose son or daughter just left home for college?
3. A businessperson?
4. A young man who is about to leave home for the first time?

5. A man in your class who is under temptation to have an extramarital affair?
6. The class member who reads his or her horoscope every day in the newspaper and takes it very seriously?

These are real-life situations. Yes, you do have members with these problems sitting in classes in your church.

The principle of sympathy and empathy

How you say something is just as important as *what* you say, but *what* class members say is not necessarily what they *mean*. We are dealing with people here, and that is how we act.

For instance, consider the following statements. In the first column is the statement as it originally appeared. In the second, what it really turned out to mean. A sharp teacher will listen for real meaning (remember what we learned about listening in the chapter on friendship evangelism) and then show sympathy and empathy in dealing with the person making the statement.

Occasion	Statement	Real Meaning
A parent-teacher conference at a school	"Your son, Johnny, is an underachiever, and his marks are low because he lacks motivation."	"Johnny spends too much time in front of the TV and is stupid and lazy."
A news item in the local paper	Ten additional sanitation operatives were hired by the municipal motorized environmental control agency.	The city's street-cleaning department hired ten more garbage collectors.
Announcement at a staff meeting.	"We regret to inform you that Mr. Roxwell is no longer with us."	Roxwell got drunk and at ninety m.p.h., rammed his Miata under a truck trailer.

This principle also applies to how you approach certain topics when you give a Bible study. Ellen White makes a very significant statement about how to approach doctrinal issues:

> In bearing the message, make no personal thrusts at other churches, not even the Roman Catholic Church. Angels of God see in the different denominations many who can be reached only by the greatest caution. Therefore, let us be careful of our words. . . . Speak the truth in tones and words of love. Let Jesus Christ be exalted. Keep to the affirmation of truth. Never leave the straight path God has marked out, for the purpose of giving someone a thrust. That thrust may do much harm and no good. It may quench conviction in many minds.[6]

Bobby Allen revisited

Remember my experience with Bobby Allen? Let's see if we can do it better.

Assume for a minute that you are a Roman Catholic, and an Adventist is studying with you. Which of the following brief Bible-study outlines on the change of the Sabbath to Sunday do you think most closely follows Ellen White's advice and uses the principle of sympathy and empathy? (See next page.) Notice the language and approach in each study. (These are actual Bible studies taken from Adventist sources).

Both studies teach the truth. They do not skirt the issue. Both are very clear on what happened, but one is kinder than the other in the language it uses and its approach to the subject. I have personally seen both these studies in action, and Study 2 always wins more converts than Study 1, simply because it teaches truth without erecting psychological barriers that then have to be overcome.

Please note: Being kind and empathetic does not mean that you water down truth. It just means that you attempt to teach truth without antagonizing people.

The principle of correlation

The principle of correlation means that the teacher will find

Study 1	Study 2

Intro.: Sunday bears the mark of paganism. We will discover in our study of the prophecies that what we see in Christianity today is the result of a subtle campaign by the "prince of this world" to substitute his day for God's day.
 	
  I. Prophecy shows that an attempt would be made to change the law of God.
     A. The papacy is the "man of sin" and the "little horn."
 II. The rise of the papacy
     A. The true head of the church.
     B. Where did the apostasy begin?
     C. The spirit of exaltation.
     D. The exaltation of the bishop of Rome.
III. The exaltation of the day of the sun
IV. The Roman Catholic Church admits to its participation in the change
 V. Sunday is of human origin
     A. Its origin is in the "mystery of iniquity"
 	
Conclusion: Obey God by doing His will.
	Intro.: Astronomy governs days, months, and years, but there is no basis in astronomy for the week. It was established by God in the beginning.
	
	  I. The apostolic sabbath
	     A. Jesus, the law, and the Sabbath
	     B. The blessed Virgin Mary and the Sabbath
	     C. The apostles and the Sabbath
	 II. Emperor Constantine misleads the church with a different day
	III. Review of the events during the time of Constantine
	     A. The identity of the papacy as the little horn becomes self-evident as the study progresses. People draw their own conclusions.
	
	Conclusion: Hebrews 4:9. A rest (Sabbath) remains for the people of God. This is a serious matter that demands a serious decision.

a way to bring all the facts together *so that people can see the big picture.*

A lot of teaching is done by bits and pieces. In fact, most people think in bits and pieces. It is difficult for us to get it together, so it is up to the teacher to make sure the pieces all fall into place.

For instance, most Sabbath School lessons are thirteen pieces of one topic. What's the topic? Many Sabbath School class members don't know. They never get the big picture. They never make the connection.

The parable of the sower

Notice how Jesus used the principle of correlation in the parable of the sower (see Matthew 13:1-23). If you had been walking down the road, you might have seen a bird or two and a scraggly plant struggling for existence between a couple of rocks, and that would have probably been it.

Jesus, however, said, "The kingdom of heaven is like . . ." That starts a correlation—putting it all together.

Then He said, "The seed along the path is . . ."; "the seed among the rock is . . ." The disciples began to get the big picture. By the time He finished, they had gotten it.

Jesus used an agricultural illustration they could relate to. He went from the known, the actual incident, to the unknown, the meaning of the story, and it correlated. The disciples said, in effect, "Oh, now we get it . . . !"

In other words, when you teach, shoot at a target; don't just shoot.

---

1. Look in your pastor's library, and you will likely see how-to books in each of these areas.
2. *Gospel Workers*, 407.
3. *Evangelism*, 338.
4. *Spiritual Advancement the Object of Camp-Meetings*, 1897, 41. This is a pamphlet included on the Ellen White Writings CD-ROM produced by the White Estate.
5. W. E. Vine, *The Expanded Vine's Expository Dictionary of New Testament Words* (Minneapolis: Bethany House Publishers, 1984).
6. *Evangelism*, 576.

CHAPTER 8

Live Saints in a Pagan World

Let's face it—it's a jungle out there! This is not a friendly world. It is filled with riots, civil wars, drive-by shootings, child molestation cases, and carjackings. Half the marriages in North America end in divorce. Drugs are everywhere. Gangs move from cities to small towns, creating new markets for the drug trade. Unprovoked attacks by one ethnic group on another leave a trail of innocent victims littering the streets.

I can guarantee you that whoever wrote that America's "alabaster cities gleam undimmed by human tears" didn't live in this neighborhood!

Not long ago I was at an evening meeting at a church. We finished around 9:00 p.m. As I was leaving for the parking lot, I was suddenly surrounded by a phalanx of deacons.

"What's up?" I asked.

"Pastor, we are your escort. In this neighborhood, you don't go to the parking lot by yourself."

Vote my way—or else!

You think this doesn't affect the church? Think again. A leading officer in a church had come up with some theological ideas that were not acceptable. He went through the process of presenting his ideas to various levels of church entities, and the time had come to meet in a church business meeting and let the congregation know that his teachings were not correct.

The final action taken by the church, a wise one, was to allow him to retain his church membership, but to relieve him of his duties as a church officer and request that he study with a group of experts for a period of two months to see if it could help him get his thinking straightened out.

The next day, we learned that this man had a squad of armed cohorts surrounding the church ready to shoot the conference officials should the vote go entirely against him. When confronted, his answer was, "Hey, an eye for an eye, the Bible says!" No wonder the apostle Paul says:

> But mark this: There will be terrible times in the last days. People will be lovers of themselves, lovers of money, boastful, proud, abusive, disobedient to their parents, ungrateful, unholy, without love, unforgiving, slanderous, without self-control, brutal, not lovers of the good, treacherous, rash, conceited, lovers of pleasure rather than lovers of God—having a form of godliness but denying its power (2 Timothy 3:1-5).

No wonder Paul admonishes Christians to put on the whole armor of God (see Ephesians 6:11). You need to be armor-clad out there. It's the only way to survive in a hostile world.

This is the kind of world you and I live in. This is the kind of world in which we are called to live as committed, dedicated Christians.

Building a sanctification model

Every Christian, whether he or she realizes it or not, has a way, a pattern, for living a Christian life in the midst of a hostile world. To have a handle to hang on to, we'll call this pattern a sanctification model.

A sanctification model is built by a person examining what the Bible says about Christian living and then constructing a lifestyle around that information.

In this chapter we'll look at some elements that must be included. There are more, but this chapter is too short to include them all.[1] First, however, let's take a look at some popular sanctification models we see in action around us.

The great saint model

Some people build and use sanctification models that are completely personalized. That means someone invents his or her own model, and only the one who invented it knows how it works. When a person does this, he or she will automatically assume that everyone else: (1) knows what his or her personal sanctification model is and (2) will live up to it. The problem with this kind of model is that it all too often becomes judgmental and legalistic.

This is what the Pharisees did, and Jesus had little use for their model. "Woe to you, teachers of the law and Pharisees," Jesus said, "you hypocrites! You give a tenth of your spices— mint, dill and cummin. But you have neglected the more important matters of the law—justice, mercy and faithfulness. You should have practiced the latter, without neglecting the former" (Matthew 23:23).

The Pharisees' model didn't do much for new converts, either: "Woe to you, teachers of the law and Pharisees, you hypocrites! You travel over land and sea to win a single convert, and when he becomes one, you make him twice as much a son of hell as you are" (Matthew 23:15).

This great saint model inevitably produces the Great Saint syndrome described by Isaiah: " 'Keep away; don't come near me, for I am too sacred for you!' " (Isaiah 65:5).

Here's a personality profile of a person suffering from Great Saint syndrome:

Theological Emphasis—Almost exclusively on sanctification.

Sociological Emphasis—"I am he [or she]."

Attitude—"Keep away; don't come near me, for I am too sacred for you!"

Motivation—Guilt and duty.

Favorite Words—"Don't," and "Ellen White says..." (whether she does or not!).

Favorite Face—Long.

The staged holiness model

Another sanctification model popular in today's world grew out of the ministry of John Wesley. It is alternatively called "entire sanctification," "second blessing," "perfect love," "Christian holiness," and, in its Pentecostal mode, "the baptism of the Holy Spirit," or the "baptism of fire."

According to this idea, there are two or three distinct and identifiable stages to the process of salvation. The first is justification and the new birth, which kicks in the process of sanctification, and the second is a "second blessing," which occurs at some point subsequent to the new birth. The second blessing, or entire sanctification, is a work of the Holy Spirit that removes most of the effects of original sin.[2] For instance, Article X of the Constitution of the Church of the Nazarene, a staunch upholder of this idea, says:

> We believe that entire sanctification is the act of God, subsequent to regeneration, by which believers are made free from original sin, or depravity, and brought into a state of entire devotment to God, and the holy obedience of love made perfect.[3]

Many, if not most, Pentecostal denominations and churches follow this model and add a third stage, called the baptism of the Holy Spirit, or the baptism of fire. According to this concept, people know when they become entirely sanctified because they speak in tongues. This is why many Pentecostal organizations call themselves "full gospel."[4]

There have been, and still are, movements within Adventism that sway in this direction, though this view has never been officially part of Adventist theology or lifestyle.[5]

The sun-and-sand view

There is yet another view of sanctification that is not unknown to Seventh-day Adventist circles. This is the idea that a true Christian life can only be attained by pulling out of society and going to live in some remote commune with like-minded people. This ascetic (lonely and isolated) lifestyle will somehow produce the desired degree of holiness. This is sometimes referred to as "country living."[6]

I have called this the sun-and-sand view because many people who follow it have a great deal in common with a group of early church people known as the "desert fathers." These were people who separated themselves from the world, lived in the deserts of North Africa, and founded what became known as the monastic movement in the Roman Catholic Church. Many ascetic movements, including Adventist ones, tend to become legalistic, extremist, and judgmental of everyone else, just as the desert fathers did.[7]

Sanctification as the work of a lifetime

Seventh-day Adventists have historically followed a model that sees sanctification as something that happens progressively over a person's lifetime. We call it Christian lifestyle, Christian living, and upholding the standards.[8] Ellen White clearly summarized our view when she stated, "There is no such thing as instantaneous sanctification. True sanctification is a daily work, continuing as long as life shall last."[9]

What does the Bible say?

Having outlined some views on sanctification and Christian lifestyle, let's see what the Bible has to say.

Two little-used texts well describe the pathway of sanctification: Proverbs 1:20-33 and Deuteronomy 30:11-14.

Proverbs 1:20-33 says, in summary, God reveals truth in life's experiences, from which some will learn. Others will not hear it and will suffer for it. Deuteronomy 30:11-14 says:

> Now what I am commanding you today is not too difficult for you or beyond your reach. It is not up in heaven, so that you have to ask, "Who will ascend into heaven to get it and proclaim it to us so we may obey it?" Nor is it beyond the sea, so that you have to ask, "Who will cross the sea to get it and proclaim it to us so we may obey it?" No, the word is very near you; it is in your mouth and in your heart so you may obey it.

Six places you find information

There are six places in the Bible where we have lists of Christian personality traits and outlines of Christian lifestyles and behavior: The Ten Commandments, the holiness code (Leviticus 17-27), a list of seven sins God hates (Proverbs 6:16-19), the Sermon on the Mount (Matthew 5-7), Peter's ladder (2 Peter 1:5-9), and the fruit of the Spirit (Galatians 5:22-26).

These six lists have one thing in common: they all deal with what pleases the Lord. *They all focus on giving glory to God because of who He is.* That is the essence of the gospel. Whatever we *do* as Christians is a legitimate part of the sanctification process only if it is for the glory of God; otherwise, it rapidly degenerates into salvation by works, whether we intend it to or not.

That is why Jesus summarized sanctification under two broad categories, both beginning with the word *love*: love the Lord your God with all your heart and with all your soul and with all your mind, and love your neighbor as yourself (see Matthew 22:36-39).

The Ten Commandments

The first four of the Ten Commandments deal with worship, and the last six with human relationships; family relationships, law and order, sexual relationships, truthfulness, property rights, and covetousness that may lead to unlawful action.

The holiness code

The holiness code in Leviticus 17-27 is a detailed list of ethical actions and social mores based on the outline of the Ten Commandments.

Seven sins God hates

The uniqueness of this list of ethical requirements is that it focuses on human relationships. These seven things the Lord hates are precisely the things that cause unending trouble between people and in churches.

The Sermon on the Mount

The Sermon on the Mount takes some well-known Old Testament ethical requirements and shows how they have been twisted out of their original shapes and superimposed on true religion in ways the Lord never intended. It also discusses some prohibited actions, such as adultery, and shows how undercover thoughts are part and parcel of overt acts.

Peter's ladder

Peter's ladder shows how certain attitudes, understandings, and perceptions are built one on the other as a way of making our "calling and election sure" (2 Peter 1:10).

The fruit of the Spirit

Galatians 5:22-26 brings it all together in one place. The character traits outlined here are the full picture of what a Christian personality is supposed to look like. This is God's ideal. It is what He takes for granted a Christian will be like:

Notice that the Bible says "fruit [singular] of the Spirit," not "fruits [plural] of the Spirit." This is not a ladder; it is a composite. All these traits are supposed to be in every Christian's personality all the time. That is a sanctified life.

You and your church

Christians do not live in a vacuum. The Lord calls us to be live saints in a pagan world.

Your local church is where that action is. You, I, and the members of our church are those saints. Our Christian example and testimony is the one people hear, see, and "read." The corporate Christian personalities of the congregations you and I belong to are the ones people within our sphere of influence hear, see, and "read."

It may be an interesting activity to study and debate the theological nuances of sanctification, but it is a lot more urgent to see it in action in you and me and in our congregations.

So let's go out there in that pagan jungle and act like live saints. Paul was right on when he wrote to Timothy, who was about to be set loose in the same kind of jungle in a city called Ephesus, "Watch your life and doctrine closely. Persevere in them, because if you do, you will save both yourself and your hearers" (1 Timothy 4:16).

---

1. If you are interested in pursuing this subject further, see Edward Heppenstall, *Salvation Unlimited* (Washington, D.C.: Review and Herald Publishing Association, 1974); Arnold Wallenkampf, *What Every Christian Should Know About Being Justified* (Washington, D.C.: Review and Herald Publishing Association, 1988); George Knight, *The Pharisee's Guide to Perfect Holiness* (Boise, Idaho: Pacific Press, 1992); and *Seventh-day Adventists Believe . . .* (Washington, D.C.: Review and Herald Publishing Association, 1988), chapter 10.
2. For an Adventist evaluation of this position, see Hans K. LaRondelle, *Perfection and Perfectionism* (Berrien Springs, Mich.: Andrews University Press, 1971).
3. W. T. Pukiser, *Sanctification and Its Synonyms* (Kansas City, Mo.: Beacon Hill Press, 1961), 88. The Church of the Nazarene still follows rather closely the original ideas of John Wesley. See, for instance, H. Orton Wiley, *Christian Theology* (Kansas City, Mo.: Beacon Hill Press, 1940).
4. See *Dictionary of Pentecostal and Charismatic Movements* (Grand Rapids: Zondervan Publishing House, 1988), s.v. "Baptism of the Holy Spirit."
5. The best known is the holy flesh movement that broke out at the turn of the century. This movement is the focus of continual discussion in Adventist circles. See the article "Holy Flesh Heresy" in the *Seventh-day Adventist Encyclopedia* (Washington, D.C.: Review and Herald Publishing Association, 1976) for a short summary of the movement. See Ellen White, *Revival and Beyond* (Washington, D.C.: Review and Herald Publishing Association, 1972) for a concise study of why we Adventists do not subscribe to holiness views of sanctification.
6. Don't mix up this view with Ellen White's call to leave the cities at a certain moment in earth's history. They use the same terminology, but they are not the same thing.
7. See William DeArteaga, *Quenching the Spirit* (Lake Mary, Fla.: Creation House, 1992). This is a book written from the viewpoint of the health-wealth wing of charismatics, so you may not agree with a lot of what the author says, but his information on the desert fathers is interesting.
8. Our handbook for this viewpoint is Ellen White's *Steps to Christ*.
9. *The Sanctified Life*, 10.

CHAPTER 9

Is Water Baptism Enough?

"I suppose," the woman said to me, "that if I join your church, I will have to 'dip'?"

We were on the same Caribbean island where the Christmas pig incident took place, and since most of the people were Roman Catholics, "dipping" was not a common mode of baptism.

"Dipping" in the sunshine

I knew the theological arguments for baptism by immersion as opposed to sprinkling or pouring, but it had never occurred to me how people get ideas about baptism mixed up with traditions and local customs, or have hang-ups about the service itself.

"If I decide to dip," she asked, "at what time of day will it happen?"

I explained that we usually baptized during our worship services, but we sometimes had afternoon services at the beach and baptized in the sea.

"All right," she said, "as long as I don't have to dip at the wrong time of day, I will think about it." I soon became aware that her concern about the time of day for the baptism had to do with catching cold or staying well when in contact with water.

As it turned out, this woman was mostly concerned with the form of the ceremony itself, not with its theological meaning.

More than a ceremony

Baptism, however, certainly ought to be more than a ceremony. According to the Bible, baptism is an important issue.

Jesus told Nicodemus that unless a person is born of water and the Spirit, he or she cannot enter the kingdom (see John 3:5), and He later said, "Whoever believes and is baptized will be saved" (Mark 16:16). You and I usually think of baptism in these theological terms. These instructions make baptism more than a ceremony. Paul says:

> What shall we say, then? Shall we go on sinning so that grace may increase? By no means! We died to sin; how can we live in it any longer? Or don't you know that all of us who were baptized into Christ Jesus were baptized into his death? We were therefore buried with him through baptism into death in order that, just as Christ was raised from the dead through the glory of the Father, we too may live a new life.
>
> If we have been united with him like this in his death, we will certainly also be united with him in his resurrection. For we know that our old self was crucified with him so that the body of sin might be rendered powerless, that we should no longer be slaves to sin (Romans 6:1-6).

But we often treat the ceremony itself with less importance. Ellen White reinforces its importance:

> Christ has made baptism the sign of entrance to His spiritual kingdom. He has made this a positive condition with which all must comply who wish to be acknowledged as under the authority of the Father, the Son, and the Holy Spirit. Before man can find a home in the church, before passing the threshold of God's spiritual kingdom, he is to receive the impress of the divine name.[1]

Three kinds of baptism

The Bible talks about three kinds of baptism: water baptism, the baptism of the Holy Spirit, and the baptism of fire.

Water baptism

Water baptism is a biblical requirement. We learn about it

partly through a study of the Greek word *baptizo* and partly through illustrations of how and when it was done in Bible times.[2]

The Gospels tell us about the baptizing activities of John the Baptist and Jesus' disciples (see John 4:1, 2).

The book of Acts tells about various people being baptized: three thousand on the Day of Pentecost (see Acts 2:41), some Samaritans (see Acts 8:12), an Ethiopian (see Acts 8:36), Paul, shortly after his conversion (see Acts 9:18), Cornelius and his household (see Acts 10:47), and many other converts (see Acts 16-22).

Paul mentions that he personally baptized some converts (see 1 Corinthians 15, 16).

Baptizing a pickle

Believe it or not, one of the best illustrations of what baptism means comes from the story of the baptism of a pickle! Please don't close this book yet—let me explain.

There are two forms of a Greek word used for *baptism*. One is *baptizo*, which means "to submerge," as when a ship sinks. *Baptizo* comes from *bapto*, which is the basic word meaning "to dip."

Baptizo has a more complex meaning than the core word *bapto*. *Baptizo* contains the idea that after the dipping, some permanent change takes place. That's where the pickle comes in.

A Greek poet and physician, Nicander, who lived about 200 B.C., recorded a recipe for making pickles that uses both words. Nicander says that in order to make a pickle, the vegetable should first be "dipped" (*bapto*) into boiling water and then "baptized" (*baptizo*) in the vinegar solution. Both verbs involve the immersing of vegetables in a solution. The first immersion in boiling water, however, is temporary. The second immersion, the act of "baptizing" the vegetable in the vinegar solution, produces a permanent change.[3]

Jesus combined these two ideas when He said, "Whoever believes and is baptized will be saved" (Mark 16:16). Baptism as a ceremony (*bapto*), or just mental assent to a set of doctrines, is not enough. Baptism includes union with Jesus, a real change in thinking, attitude, and lifestyle (*baptizo*).

Making baptism memorable

Every baptismal service in your church ought to be a major event. It is one of the most important ceremonies in the life of the church.

All too often a baptism is just tacked on at the beginning or end of a worship service, as if it were a relatively unimportant appendage.

The case of the baptismal dress

The other side of this coin, however, is that sometimes the outward accouterments of the service become more important than its meaning, however unintentionally. Cultural ideas and traditions can actually short-circuit the deep significance of baptism.

One of our church members studied with a woman, and she decided to join the church. The day of her baptism arrived, and everything was ready, except that near the end of Sabbath School that morning she had not yet shown up.

The head elder and I went to her house and found her in tears. "You people," she said, "did not prepare me well for baptism, and now I have to change my mind."

My first thought was that she had come across some doctrinal issue she didn't understand. "Please tell us where we failed. Is there something we can study some more? Is there some teaching of the church you discovered you don't understand?"

"Oh, no," she replied, "I don't have any problem with the church's teachings. It's just that I don't have a white dress!

"Some sisters from the church came by to help me get ready for the baptism," she said, "but when they discovered I didn't have a white dress, they told me that I couldn't be baptized until I had one, and I can't afford it."

Wearing a white dress was normal procedure in that area of the world, and the women from the church were just trying to be helpful. In talking with them later, they said they never realized that this custom might impede the woman from being baptized. We resolved the problem, and the woman was baptized, but it taught us all a lesson: The form of the ceremony should never override its meaning.

The baptism of the Holy Spirit

Nicander's pickle recipe also gives us some insight into the baptism of the Holy Spirit, something we Adventists don't talk much about.

As mentioned in chapter 3, we tend to allow our opposition to Pentecostalism to color our thinking too much. It was Jesus Himself who said that we would be baptized with the Holy Spirit (see Acts 1:5), so let's see what the Bible says about it.

What the baptism of the Holy Spirit is not

First, let's clear up what it is not. The baptism of the Holy Spirit is not a so-called second work of grace. You may want to review what was said in chapter 8 on this subject.[4] The baptism of the Holy Spirit is not speaking in tongues. We don't have space in this chapter to discuss this issue, but you can get some good books on the subject at your local ABC.[5]

Power to the wheels

The baptism of the Holy Spirit is an empowerment for service. It is what makes the mission enterprise of the church function effectively. It works on the converted mind and heart and builds in new concepts and new vision. Notice a significant statement from Ellen White:

> The Spirit of God, as it comes into the heart by faith, is the beginning of the life eternal. *With the baptism of the Holy Spirit* upon the teacher of truth, he can talk of Christ and Him crucified in language that savors of heaven. *The mind and spirit of Christ will be in him, and he can present the will of God to man because his own heart has been brought into submission, and has been glorified by the Spirit of God.* The Sun of Righteousness is risen upon him, that he might reflect its brightness to the world, and he will give evidence in a holy life that the truth he has received has been a sanctifying principle, and not a mere theory.[6]

The key Bible text about the baptism of the Holy Spirit is Acts 1:8: "But you will receive power when the Holy Spirit comes on you, and you will be my witnesses."

Two experiences in the Bible point this out. The first is the experience of the Day of Pentecost.

In the upper room, Peter got the idea of reorganizing the church (see Acts 1:15-26). He focused on the Old Testament pattern of twelve and felt it was necessary (verse 21) to reestablish this pattern from among the eyewitnesses (verse 22). They did it, using an Old Testament system of casting lots, and chose Matthias.

Then, as Acts 2:2 points out, "suddenly" the Holy Spirit arrived. It empowered them instantaneously (see Acts 2:4). Peter's reorganization scheme disappeared, along with Matthias. All of a sudden, the disciples were out on the street preaching and making converts. That is the baptism of the Holy Spirit.[7]

The second experience took place in the city of Ephesus (see Acts 19). Paul found some disciples of John the Baptist there who knew nothing about the Holy Spirit. He explained it to them, and the power arrived. The next thing you know, they were out on the streets, and the whole city and the surrounding provinces knew about Christianity. Empowerment for service— that's the key.

When does it happen?

The baptism of the Holy Spirit ought to happen before water baptism, or at least at the same time (see John 3:5). That's what happened to Jesus Himself (see John 1:29-34). Cornelius and his family received both water baptism and the baptism of the Holy Spirit at the same time (see Acts 10:44-48).

Unfortunately, that's not always the case. For instance, Jesus' disciples received a great deal of instruction about the Holy Spirit, but their baptism didn't happen until the Day of Pentecost.

Baptism of fire

The Bible mentions a baptism of fire only once, in connection with John the Baptist's response to an inquiry as to whether he was the Messiah:

> I baptize you with water for repentance. But after me will come one who is more powerful than I, whose sandals I am not fit to carry. He will baptize you with the Holy Spirit and with fire (Matthew 3:11).

There are a number of views as to what this baptism means.[8] Some believe it is synonymous with water baptism in the sense that in the Scriptures, water and fire are both symbols of purification.[9] Others believe it is a reference to the tongues of fire on the Day of Pentecost. Yet others see it as a third work of grace evidenced by speaking in tongues and entire sanctification.[10]

In one reference, Ellen White equates this baptism with the prophecy of the golden bowls and the oil in Zechariah 4. The oil represents the Holy Spirit and the golden bowls the hearts of the messengers, who are both empowered and given zeal to preach the message:

> These empty themselves into the golden bowls, which represent the hearts of the living messengers of God, who bear the Word of the Lord to the people in warnings and entreaties. The Word itself must be as represented, the golden oil, emptied from the two olive trees that stand by the Lord of the whole earth. This is the baptism by the Holy Spirit with fire. This will open the soul of unbelievers to conviction. The wants of the soul can be met only by the working of the Holy Spirit of God. Man can of himself do nothing to satisfy the longings and meet the aspirations of the heart.[11]

In another reference, she again equates it with the zeal manifested by the early disciples as a result of the baptism of the Holy Spirit.[12]

Her view is supported by a short statement by Paul in 1 Thessalonians 5:19: "Do not put out the Spirit's fire." This is a reference to testing the gift of prophecy and holding on to what is correct, adding credence to the fire as the content of the message combined with the zeal of the messenger.

Putting the three baptisms together

Water baptism is a gospel requirement because it symbolizes in a public ceremony the death and burial of an old life and resurrection to a new. It is a personal testimony in a public forum to the renewal, regeneration, and new birth that have taken place in a person's life.

The baptism of the Holy Spirit empowers for service. It ought to take place in conjunction with renewal, regeneration, and new birth. If it doesn't, it truncates the new-birth experience, and the water-baptism service becomes only a partial and incomplete testimony.

On a personal level, the baptism of fire, another facet of the same renewal, regeneration, and new-birth process, adds zeal and daring to a person's witness. It does just what it did on the Day of Pentecost when it turned confused, conservative, backward-looking disciples into dynamic, creative, daring witnesses.

On a congregational level, the baptism of fire revives dreary church services and converts them into dynamic soul-winning and soul-sustaining tools of the Spirit. Ellen White puts it right on the line:

There is no reason why our lips should not be trained to the high praises of God. When we hear the words of a cheering discourse, or the earnest exhortation of a brother or sister, why should not a wave of glory and a chorus of "Amens" go up to God from the congregation of His people? Would it not be thus if the fire of God's love were kindled in our hearts? I know it would be so. Coldness, formality, want of faith and love and intense earnestness and devotion, has killed the spirit of warmth and religion out of our services. We need everything,—the gold of love, the white raiment, which is the righteousness of Christ, the eye-salve,—that we may discern the goodness and love of God. When God works for His people, how few return to give

Him glory? We want a religion that has some consolation in it, that has joy and peace and love in it to recommend it to others. Our religion should be of that heavenly character that will impress the world with the fact that we have been with Jesus and have learned of Him.[13]

So let's get some power to the wheels, Adventists. Time to trade in the Model Ts for 3000 GTs. It's power that gets the space shuttles into orbit, and it's power that moves the church. Get out there and shout. We have a message, and time is running out.

1. *The Faith I Live By*, 145.

2. For an interesting study of early baptismal services, see Henry F. Brown, *Baptism Through the Centuries* (Mountain View, Calif.: Pacific Press Publishing Association, 1965).

3. James Montgomery Boice, *Bible Study Magazine*, May 1989.

4. For an extensive study on this issue in the Pentecostal tradition, see *Dictionary of Pentecostal and Charismatic Movements* (Grand Rapids, Mich.: Zondervan Publishing House, 1988), s.v. "Baptism in the Holy Spirit."

5. For an autobiographical account of a person who came to believe this, see Frederick K. C. Price, *The Holy Spirit the Missing Ingredient: My Personal Testimony* (Tulsa, Okla.: Harrison House, 1978). For the Adventist view on this issue, see John Robertson, *Tongues: What You Should Know About Glossolalia* (Boise, Idaho.: Pacific Press Publishing Association, 1977); Nicholas Fisher, *Understanding Tongues* (England: Stanborough Press Limited, n.d.); Morris L. Venden, *Your Friend, The Holy Spirit* (Boise, Idaho.: Pacific Press Publishing Association, 1986).

6. *Bible Echo* and *Signs of the Times*, March 1, 1892, emphasis mine.

7. For a training course on how this can happen in your church, see Garrie F. Williams, *How to Be Filled With the Holy Spirit and Know It* (Hagerstown, Md.: Review and Herald Publishing Association, 1991).

8. *SDA Bible Commentary* cites a number of views, but takes no position (see vol. 5, p. 300, s.v. "Fire").

9. LeRoy E. Froom, *The Coming of the Comforter* (Washington, D.C.: Review and Herald Publishing Association, 1931), 269.

10. See *Dictionary of Pentecostal and Charismatic Movements* (Grand Rapids, Mich.: Zondervan Publishing House, 1988), s.v. "Fire-baptized Holiness Church."

11. MS 109, 1897 (*SDA Bible Commentary*, 4:1180).

12. See *Bible Training School*, 1 Jan. 1911.

13. *The Signs of the Times,* 6 May 1889.

CHAPTER 10

Breaking the Stained-Glass Barrier

We were in a special committee the church had set up to study our visitor-assimilation program. To make sure we were really getting the right "feel," we invited some recently baptized members to join us.

"What was it like coming into this church?" we asked them. "Was it easy to get in?"

We assumed, of course, that we were a tender, loving church that treated people very well.

"We are here," they informed us, "because we are convinced that what the church teaches is the truth, but it was not easy to get into this church."

You could have heard a pin drop!

"What does that mean?" one of the committee members asked. "We have . . ." and he went on to describe a host of activities, programs, and fellowship opportunities our church sponsored.

"It means," one of the new members said, "that you are not aware of some of the psychological and sociological barriers that exist in this church. It is hard to get 'in.' "

Stained-glass barriers

What these new members ran into is very typical. Any large group such as a congregation tends to break itself into small groupings built around similar interests, nationalities, family ties, and a host of other factors. (These are not the same as the small groups we will discuss later.) These off-the-cuff small groupings close up, erecting invisible, but very real, barriers,

93

often without realizing it, and become impenetrable to new people. The people in these groups may well be dedicated saints; they just don't "see" anyone else.

Our job is to break down these stained-glass barriers and create a different kind of atmosphere, a TLC (tender-loving-care) congregation.

Breaking the stained-glass barrier

No church can be truly successful in this day and age unless it intentionally breaks these barriers. There are three Greek words used in the New Testament that give us clues about how to organize local congregations so that these barriers no longer exist.

Koinonia is the Greek word for fellowship. *Koinonia* is translated as "fellowship" twelve times, as "communion" four times, and also once as "joint participation." *Koinonia* happens when there is a warm, unhurried, informal atmosphere in a church.

Allelon is the Greek word that is usually translated "one another" and is used in about twenty-six statements in the New Testament that paint a picture of a corporate lifestyle for a church congregation. *Allelon* gives the congregation a corporate personality that promotes *koinonia*.

Oikos is the Greek word for "house," but in the Bible it is often used in the broader sense of "household," an extended family, including friends, relatives, business associates, and anyone else within a person's sphere of influence.

Oikos is the system through which an *allelon*-oriented congregation reaches out to bring other people into its *koinonia*.

Now that we are all experts in Greek, let's see how, using these three concepts as a basis, it is possible to build a system in a church that adequately eliminates stained-glass barriers and builds a congregation characterized by TLC.

What is the biblical model?

There are biblical models to guide us. Two passages of Scripture, the book of Ephesians and Acts 2:42-47, best illustrate the biblical model.

Ephesians 3:10 says that God intends to make His truth

known through the church. "The church," in this case, is you and me, not a building or an institution. To do this, we are individually given power through the ministry of the Holy Spirit (see Ephesians 3:15, 16). The way to retain this power is by putting on the whole armor of God (see Ephesians 6:11). This leads to a "bond of peace" (Ephesians 4:3) that results in "one body and one Spirit . . . one Lord, one faith, one baptism" (Ephesians 4:4, 5).

Ellen White points us to this model:

> In the fourth chapter of Ephesians the plan of God is so plainly and simply revealed that all His children may lay hold upon the truth. Here the means which He has appointed to keep unity in His church, that its members may reveal to the world *a healthy religious experience*, is plainly declared.[1]

Acts 2:42-47 describes what a TLC church looks like:

> They devoted themselves to the apostles' teaching and to the fellowship, to the breaking of bread and to prayer. Everyone was filled with awe, and many wonders and miraculous signs were done by the apostles. All the believers were together and had everything in common. Selling their possessions and goods, they gave to anyone as he had need. Every day they continued to meet together in the temple courts. They broke bread in their homes and ate together with glad and sincere hearts, praising God and enjoying the favor of all the people. And the Lord added to their number daily those who were being saved.

Right teachings, right atmosphere

Putting a high degree of fellowship into the church program does not in any way water down the doctrinal teachings of the church. It does, however, create an atmosphere that makes teaching the doctrines much easier and more effective.

Koinonia—TLC in action

How can a biblical model of *koinonia* become a reality in your church? It is done primarily by organizing effectively three things: your visitor system, your worship service, and your small-group ministry.

Koinonia and orange juice in Sabbath School

Before we look at these three elements, we should point out that not everyone wants a TLC church. Tradition has an incredible hold on us, especially when we invent our own traditions and then turn them into self-imposed doctrines.

We once began a half-hour fellowship time at nine on Sabbath morning, where we served orange juice, bagels, croissants, etc., and just spent the time "*koinonia*-ing." One member didn't like it.

"It is not right," he said, "to eat breakfast in church!"

"What about potluck after church?" I asked. "I see you there quite regularly."

"That's OK," he responded, "because we do that all the time, and church is over, but you can't eat at the church before church!"

I leave you to draw your own conclusions on this one!

Your visitor system

First of all, let's change the vocabulary and call visitors guests. This is a shift in attitude. A visitor might be an interloper that you would rather not have around. A guest honors us with his or her presence.

Many churches have dynamic systems for caring for guests; others don't do so well.

A friend of mine was invited to speak at a church where no one knew him personally. He arrived for Sabbath School, but there were no greeters at the door. They were all in a tight little knot off in one corner, talking and having a good time. A lot of *koinonia* was going on among church members, but at the expense of guests. My friend noticed a stack of bulletins on a table, so he took some and began handing them out at the door. Believe it or not, it was about fifteen minutes before anyone asked him who he was! That's an appalling guest system in action.

How it should work

A well-organized guest system works *by intention*. Picture yourself arriving at a church as a guest on a Sabbath morning. This church has a well-organized TLC guest system.

Someone helps you find a spot in the parking lot. Your space is near the entrance, because the members park farther out, leaving the closest spots for guests. A greeter meets you as you step out of the car, gives you some carefully chosen words of welcome, and hands you a bulletin that looks like the JCPenney catalog. It is filled with information about the church and its ministries.

The greeter notices you have two children with you, ages five and twelve. The first thing he or she does is to indicate where the restrooms are, vital information for a parent with two children. Then you are escorted to the Sabbath School activities of your choice.

You notice that all rooms are labeled with big signs, not tiny, corroded brass nameplates that look like escapees from a medieval cathedral. There are large signboards at every entrance telling where things are. There may even be a map of the campus in the bulletin.

You get the impression that this church functions with low levels of anxiety, embarrassment, and confusion. You feel at home right off the bat.

The worship service

For the worship service, you are invited to sit with a family, often in your own age bracket. The worship service includes high levels of participation. Children are highly visible, taking up the offering or singing with the musical group leading the music. Time is taken for people to talk to each other and get acquainted as part of the service. You participate in the prayers and other parts of the service.

This is called a participatory worship service. You become more than a spectator—you are part of the action.[2]

Small-group ministry

Small-group ministry means that the small-group phenomenon we described earlier is reorganized under trained leaders to be *inclusive* instead of exclusive. When this happens, small groups become a key factor in building a TLC congregation.

Small groups inherently include *koinonia*, *allelon*, and *oikos*. They are the wave of the future. How to organize them effectively is a science in itself and beyond the scope of this book. See the books listed in footnote 3 for some excellent source material on how to organize them.[3]

Allelon: corporate Christian personality

Allelon is usually translated "one another."[4] The phrases below are grouped under four headings: interrelationships; mutual edification; mutual service; and negative "one anothers." The closer a congregation comes to putting these statements into practice in its corporate life, the more it will demonstrate a Christian personality and a TLC attitude.

Interrelationships	Love one another Receive one another Greet one another Have the same care for one another Submit to one another Forbear one another Confess your sins to one another Forgive one another
Mutual Edification	Build up one another Teach one another Admonish one another Speak to one another in psalms, hymns, and spiritual songs
Mutual Service	Be servants to one another Bear one another's burdens Use hospitality to one another Be kind to one another Pray for one another

Negative "One Anothers"	Do not judge one another Do not speak evil of one another Do not murmur against one another Do not bite and devour one another Do not provoke one another Do not envy one another Do not lie to one another

The *oikos* factor

There is some evidence that the average Seventh-day Adventist in North America has a personal network of about two hundred people. This *oikos* is made up of family members, friends, acquaintances, people at work, golf companions, etc. The unchurched members of your *oikos* are the people the Lord has assigned to you to evangelize.

Your *oikos* forms a series of expanding circles, each of which is a fishing pool for converts:

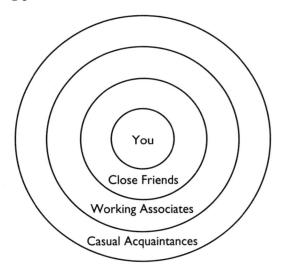

Fishing with a hook *vs.* fishing with a net

When you fish with a hook, how many fish do you catch at a

time? When you fish with a net, how many fish do you catch at a time?

Oikos relationships allow you to fish with a net. They allow you to use your time efficiently, make it easier for people to accept the gospel, and build natural bridges of assimilation into the church family.[5]

Oikos relationships provide natural networks for sharing the gospel. You don't have to go cold turkey to some unknown person. *Oikos* members are usually somewhat favorable or highly favorable on a receptivity scale. *Oikos* relationships allow unhurried and natural sharing of God's love and the gospel message. *Oikos* relationships provide natural support when a person comes to church. People ought go to church *with* someone, not alone into some mysterious, unfamiliar environment. *Oikos* relationships provide a constantly enlarging source of new contacts. New people have their own *oikos*. All you have to do is show them how to use it.

Your church doesn't need to have stained-glass barriers that keep people out. Let's take a TLC hammer and break those barriers. Turn people loose to fellowship, worship, and win souls as the Bible tells us to, and watch your church grow.

---

1. MS, *SDA Bible Commentary,* 6:1117.

2. For a good book on how to build this kind of worship service built around Adventist theological understanding, see C. Raymond Holmes, *Sing a New Song* (Berrien Springs, Mich.: Andrews University Press, 1984). You can obtain a training program that uses this book as its text from the General Conference Ministerial Association. For a unique study that examines how many churches got where they are in their worship services, see James H. Rutz, *The Open Church* (Colorado Springs: The Seedsowers, 1992). You may not agree with everything this book says, but look for the good points.

3. Monte Sahlin, *Sharing Our Faith With Friends Without Losing Either* (Hagerstown, Md.: Review and Herald Publishing Association, 1990); Miguel Cerna, *The Power of Small Groups in the Church* (Newbury Park, Calif.: El Camino Publishing, 1991); Ron Nicholas, et al., *Good Things Come in Small Groups* (Downers Grove, Ill.: InterVarsity Press, 1985); Kurt Johnson, *Small Groups Outreach* (Hagerstown, Md.: Review and Herald Publishing Association, 1991); and W. Clarence Schilt, *Dynamic Small Groups* (Hagerstown, Md.: Review and Herald Publishing Association, 1992).

4. If you are interested in more information, see Sue Harville, *Reciprocal Living* (World Team, Miami, Fl.).

5. For an *oikos* training program for your church, see James W. Zackrison, *How to Find and Reach Receptive People* (Lincoln, Neb.: NAD Distribution Center).

CHAPTER 11

Spiritual Gifts: Keys to Ministry

Once the baptism of the Holy Spirit becomes a reality in a person's life, what happens next?

Personal holiness and service

We Adventists are very much oriented toward personal holiness. Living a holy life and preparing for the time of trouble are concepts we hear about regularly in sermons, classes, books, and magazines.

Holy living is certainly important. You don't get to heaven without it.[1] On the other hand, holy living alone is only half the cake. The baptism of the Holy Spirit empowers holy living, but it also empowers for service.

The means by which this is accomplished is through the assignment of spiritual gifts to every believer by the Holy Spirit.

Prior to 1980, the fundamental beliefs of Seventh-day Adventists contained a statement regarding the gift of prophecy but were silent on all other gifts. In 1980, a specific statement of belief in all the gifts of the Spirit was added. Here is how it reads:

Fundamental Belief No. 16. God bestows upon all members of His church in every age spiritual gifts which each member is to employ in loving ministry for the common good of the church and of humanity. Given by the agency of the Holy Spirit, who apportions to each member as He wills, the gifts provide all abilities and ministries needed by the church to fulfill its divinely appointed functions.

According to the Scriptures, these gifts include such ministries as faith, healing, prophecy, proclamation, teaching, administration, reconciliation, compassion, and self-sacrificing service and charity for the help and encouragement of people. Some people are called of God and endowed with the Spirit for functions recognized by the church in pastoral, evangelistic, apostolic, and teaching ministries particularly needed to equip the members for service, to build up the church to spiritual maturity, and to foster unity of the faith and knowledge of God. When members employ these spiritual gifts as faithful stewards of God's varied grace, the church is protected from the destructive influence of false doctrine, grows with a growth that is from God, and is built up in faith and love.[2]

Are spiritual gifts still valid today?

Many churches believe that the spiritual gifts mentioned in the New Testament only functioned during the time of the early church. According to this view, when the last of the original apostles died, or when the canon of Scripture was closed, spiritual gifts were no longer needed by the church.

We Adventists maintain that this is not true for three reasons:

1. The closing of the canon of Scripture did not mark the cessation of Heaven's communication with humankind (see Joel 2:28, 29).

2. The Scriptures themselves reveal the continuing work of the Holy Spirit. Thus J. N. Andrews wrote:

Those who reject the work of the Spirit of God under the plea that the Scriptures are sufficient, do deny and reject all that part of the Bible which reveals the office and work of the Holy Spirit.[3]

3. The gift of prophecy is specifically connected with the closing work of the gospel era (see Revelation 12:17; 14:12; 19:10; Joel 2:28-32).

Ellen White indicates the importance of this subject in two statements:

> I point you to the words of the apostle Paul in the fourth chapter of Ephesians. This whole chapter is a lesson that God desires us to learn and practice.[4]

> In the fourth chapter of Ephesians the plan of God is so plainly and simply revealed that all His children may lay hold upon the truth. Here the means which He has appointed to keep unity in His church, that its members may reveal to the world a healthy religious experience, is plainly declared.[5]

What is a spiritual gift?

Dr. C. Peter Wagner offers a good definition of a spiritual gift:

> A spiritual gift is a special attribute given by the Holy Spirit to every member of the body of Christ according to God's grace for use within the context of the body.[6]

Spiritual gifts are the tools the Lord puts into the hands of the members of the church for them to use in the accomplishment of the work of the kingdom.

What the Bible says about spiritual gifts

There are four primary sources of information in the New Testament about spiritual gifts: 1 Peter 4:10; Romans 12:1-8; 1 Corinthians 12; and Ephesians 4:1-16.

First Peter 4:10 gives a comprehensive description of spiritual gifts: "Each one should use whatever gift he has received to serve others, faithfully administering God's grace in its various forms."

Romans 12:1-6 explains what "God's grace in its various forms" means. Verses 1 to 3 point out that spiritual gifts are the hedges against "thinking more highly than [one] ought" of oneself, because they give us a *measure of faith* by which to gauge ourselves. Verses 4 and 5 explain how to measure that faith—

through the use of varied gifts. Thus, the word *faith* in this text refers not only to a personal spiritual quality, but also to a *measure of function* within the corporate body of the church. This means that all gifts are important and necessary. They are all functions of one "body" and therefore of equal importance. There is no hierarchy of gifts, only differences of function.

So according to Romans 12:1-6, the spiritual gifts we receive become the framework around which we build a ministry that will serve the corporate body of the church.

Ellen White comments: "God has set in the church different gifts. These gifts are precious in their proper places, and all may act a part in the work of preparing a people for Christ's soon coming."[7]

Is this really an important issue?

I know what you're thinking—I have been sitting here in the church for many years, and I never heard much about this business of spiritual gifts before. Now you are telling me that these gifts are the framework around which I am supposed to build a ministry? Is this really all that important?

Look up 1 Corinthians 12:1. Notice what Paul says: "Now about spiritual gifts, brothers, I do not want you to be ignorant." Turn back to pages 30 and 31, and reread the two statements by Ellen White. Does this sound like an important issue to you?

How many Christians receive spiritual gifts?

There are those who believe that only clergy or ordained ministers receive spiritual gifts. Others believe that only special people such as prophets or administrators receive these gifts. Still others believe that spiritual gifts accompany an office in the church, so when you are named or elected to that office, you automatically receive a special "measure of faith" that you didn't have before.

According to the Bible, however, *all* Christians receive spiritual gifts.

Who decides who gets which gifts?

People also have different ideas about this question. Some

think the church decides who gets which gift. Others think that election to church office automatically generates the gift needed to perform that particular church function. Some think that every Christian has all the gifts; they just have to put them into practice.

None of these views is correct. First Corinthians 12:11 indicates that the Holy Spirit assigns spiritual gifts *as He decides*. The allocation of the gifts is entirely a work of the Holy Spirit.

The relationship between gifts, the Holy Spirit, and church authority

This is a critical issue because it has to do with spiritual authority within the church. Notice carefully the following quotation from Ellen White:

> Not . . . all the gifts are imparted to each believer. The Spirit divides "to every man [person] severally as he will" [1 Cor. 12:11]. But the gifts of the Spirit are promised to every believer *according to his need for the Lord's work.*[8]

Spiritual gifts are promised "according to his or her *need for the Lord's work.*" The highest authority in the church is the Holy Spirit. If the Holy Spirit assigns you a gift to use, the church cannot dictate one way or the other about your use of it, as long as it is used legitimately.

On the other hand, these gifts are given "for the Lord's work," not to make people think "more highly" of themselves than they ought (Romans 12:3).

Therefore, the authority that comes with the gifts is the authority *to do the work of the kingdom*. It does not give a person the right to exercise some kind of self-authorized imperial authority and demand this or that and in general throw his or her weight around in the church and make everybody miserable. That is why Ellen White also writes, "God dispenses His gifts as it pleases Him. He bestows one gift upon one, and another gift upon another, but all for *the good of the whole body.*"[9]

Spiritual gifts are tools with which to accomplish the work of the kingdom. They are not measures of spiritual quality, nor are they indications of positions in a chain of command.

Do spiritual gifts need to be developed?

Look up Ephesians 4:12-16. These verses talk about an experience of becoming mature (verse 13) and no longer being "infants" (verse 14).

Three things are mentioned about this process:

1. We reach unity in the faith. So according to this, faith has to be built up.
2. We reach unity in knowledge. So according to this, knowledge has to be built up.
3. By building up these two things, we become mature.

Spiritual gifts are not given to newborn Christians as "adult" gifts. Once you identify your gifts, they must be developed through use, training, and consistent discipleship.

Do spiritual gifts have anything to do with Christian personality?

Christian personality is the "music" non-Christians hear us play, as we studied in chapter 8. If people do not hear that music, they will probably not be interested in seeing just the notes on the pages of what we teach.

How does this relate to spiritual gifts?

Let's go back to Romans 12:1-3. Notice that presenting "your bodies as living sacrifices" (verse 1) involves more than healthful living. It indicates the Lord's ideal of a Christian personality, one that functions with a transformed mind, knows how to discern the will of God, does not think more highly of itself than is legitimate, and exercises sober judgment.

An unchristian personality can nullify the effective use of spiritual gifts. If you have the gift of evangelism, for instance, but you are mean or crude in your way of talking to people, they will not listen to the evangel you are trying to communicate. If you have the gift of organization and administration, but your personality leads you to a dictatorial, uncaring leadership style, your gifts will be of little use for the advancement of the kingdom.

What are the gifts mentioned in the Bible?

Twenty gifts are mentioned directly, and seven are alluded to.[10] The following chart indicates what they are:

Rom. 12	1 Cor. 12	Eph. 4
Prophecy	Prophecy	Prophecy
Teaching	Teaching	Teaching
Service	Service	Apostle
Giving	Wisdom	Evangelist
Leadership	Knowledge	Pastor
Mercy	Faith	
	Healing	
	Miracles	
	Discerning of spirits	
	Tongues	
	Interpretation of tongues	
	Helps	
	Administration	

Gifts Alluded To

Text	Gift
1 Cor. 7:7	Celibacy
1 Cor. 13:3	Voluntary poverty
1 Cor. 13:3	Martyrdom
1 Peter 4:9	Hospitality
Acts 8:5-8	Exorcism
Acts 12:12	Intercessory prayer
Rom. 11:13	Missionary

Clusters of Gifts

To make it easier to see where various gifts fit into the life and ministry of the church, Dr. Roy Naden of Andrews University proposes the following clusters:

Support Cluster	Hospitality, Helps, Service, Mercy, Giving, Intercessory prayer
Counselor Cluster	Discernment, Exhortation, Wisdom, Knowledge, Teaching
Teacher Cluster	Knowledge, Teaching
Shepherd/Evangelist Cluster	Evangelism, Pastor, Prophecy, Missionary, Apostleship
Leader Cluster	Leadership, Administration, Faith
Sign Cluster	Voluntary poverty, Martyrdom, Miracles, Healing, Exorcism, Celibacy, Tongues, Interpretation of tongues

Identifying your gifts

Sometimes it is clearly apparent what your spiritual gifts are. You can easily recognize where and how the Lord wants you to minister, and you may have been doing so for years. This is especially true of those who have the gifts of evangelism and intercessory prayer.

On the other hand, you may never have recognized what your gifts are. Maybe you have been serving the church faithfully in some role but were never very happy in what you were doing. Somehow you felt you ought to be doing something else. If this is the case, it may be that you are working outside your appointed gift mix.

A four-step process

This critical act of identifying and verifying your spiritual gifts is a four-step process.

Step One: Take a spiritual-gifts inventory. A spiritual-gifts inventory asks you questions about your experiences in the church and in religious matters. Its purpose is to discover what you have been doing or what you feel the Lord has called you to do for the advancement of the kingdom. An inventory is not exactly a test, because there are no right and wrong answers. It is a tool to help you identify your gifts.

There are several inventories available:

Wagner-Modified Houts Questionnaire.[11] This is a very complete inventory that sticks as close to the Bible as possible in identifying and testing for all the gifts mentioned or alluded to in the New Testament. You can obtain from the same source a textbook by Dr. C. Peter Wagner, *Your Spiritual Gifts Can Help Your Church Grow*, along with a set of videos that takes you through the book and the inventory.

Roy Naden, *Your Spiritual Gifts: The New Spiritual Gifts Inventory.* This inventory was developed at Andrews University and is available at your ABC or through the North American Division Distribution Center. This inventory has been carefully correlated using accepted educational testing methods so that the results are very accurate. It groups the gifts into the clusters we listed above, but it does not test for the so-called power or sign gifts.

Bobby Clinton, *Spiritual Gifts.*[12] This is the most complete study guide available on spiritual gifts. If you want to do an in-depth study of the subject, this is the book. It includes an inventory of gifts and a system for matching gifts to roles in the church.

Step Two: Have the body of the church affirm your gift. There are three reasons for this step: (1) to affirm that you really do have the gifts you think you have; (2) to make you accountable for their use; and (3) to let the church know what gifts it has as a corporate body.

If you think you have a certain spiritual gift and are trying to exercise it, but no one else in your church perceives that you have it, you probably don't.

Accountability is related to discipleship. Identifying spiritual gifts is not just an interesting activity. Gifts are identified so they will be used. For instance, if you have the gift of evangelism, and no one else knows about it, you may choose not to use it, and no one would know the difference (except the Lord, who will ultimately hold you accountable!). But once your gift is known and confirmed by the body, you are responsible for learning how to use it well and are accountable to the body for putting it into action, assuming, of course, that your church is using a system of spiritual gifts as its organizational plan.

Ideally, nominating committees ought to match church offices to spiritual gifts, not, as is all too often the case, simply to people's availability, social standing, degree of affluence, or the aggressiveness of their personalities.[13] Every church ought to have an evaluation system for measuring performance. Congregations ought to take seriously Ellen White's statement:

> If we see no necessity for harmonious action, and are disorderly, undisciplined, and disorganized in our course of action, angels, who are thoroughly organized and move in perfect order, cannot work for us successfully. They turn away in grief, for they are not authorized to bless confusion, distraction, and disorganization. All who desire the cooperation of the heavenly messengers must work in unison with them.
>
> Those who have the unction from on high will in all their efforts encourage order, discipline, and union of action, and then the angels of God can cooperate with them. But never, never will these heavenly messengers place their endorsement upon irregularity, disorganization, and disorder. All these evils are the result of Satan's efforts to weaken our forces, to destroy our courage, and prevent successful action.[14]

Step Three: Have the Lord confirm your gifts through prayer. James 1:5 says, "If any of you lacks wisdom, he should ask God, who gives generously to all without finding fault, and it will be given him." Through intercessory prayer, ask God to confirm your gifts, and He will do it. In some tangible way, you will receive the answer.

Step Four: Experiment—use your gifts in a ministry. Spiritual gifts are task oriented. That is, they are tools to do the work of the kingdom. If God has given you a gift, it is because He wants you to accomplish something for Him in the context of the body of Christ.

Spiritual gifts are the framework within which the Holy Spirit carries forward the work of the kingdom. When true gifts are in operation, whatever is supposed to happen will happen. This is your chance to identify your gifts and make your discipleship and ministry count for the Lord.

---

1. For some excellent information on personal holiness as it relates to the end time, the final generation, and the 144,000, see Marvin Moore, *The Crisis of the End Time* (Boise, Idaho: Pacific Press Publishing Association, 1992), and George R. Knight, *The Pharisee's Guide to Perfect Holiness* (Boise, Idaho: Pacific Press Publishing Association, 1992).

2. *SDA Church Manual*, 28.

3. *Review and Herald*, 15 Feb. 1870.

4. MS 55, 1903, *SDA Bible Commentary*, 6:1117.

5. MS 67, 1907, *SDA Bible Commentary*, 6:1117.

6. C. Peter Wagner, *Your Spiritual Gifts Can Help Your Church Grow* (Ventura, Calif.: Regal Books, 1979).

7. *Gospel Workers*, 481.

8. *The Desire of Ages*, 823, emphasis mine.

9. *Counsels to Teachers*, 315.

10. This chapter is too short to include material on how to identify your gifts and convert them into ministries. If you are interested in pursuing this topic further, see James W. Zackrison, *Spiritual Gifts: Keys to Ministry* (available through the NAD Distribution Center), and Roy C. Naden, *Your Spiritual Gifts: Making the Great Discovery* (Berrien Springs, Mich.: Instructional Product Development, 1989). This series contains a set of videotapes, a book, and a workbook.

11. Charles E. Fuller Institute of Evangelism and Church Growth, P.O. Box 91990, Pasadena, CA 91109.

12. Horizon House Publishers, Drawer AA, Cathedral City, CA 92234.

13. A notebook of job descriptions matched to spiritual gifts is available at your ABC. See James W. Zackrison, *Spiritual Gifts: Keys to Ministry* (available through the NAD Distribution Center) for the description of a system for doing this very thing.

14. *Testimonies for the Church*, 1:649, 650.

CHAPTER 12

Evangelism Is Alive and Well on Planet Earth

"One thing we want to make clear," the head elder said during an interview, "if you come to this church as our pastor, we do not want to hear the word *evangelism* from you." Seems strange that a Seventh-day Adventist pastor would come face to face with such an attitude, but it's not an isolated case by any means. *Evangelism* is a bad word in some circles.

"The problem with your congregation," my fellow pastor remarked, "is that you don't do any evangelism. If you did, your church wouldn't be dead." The interesting thing is that attendance in my church went from around seventy-five to over three hundred in a couple of years, and we were actively involved in all kinds of things. We had not, however, held a public evangelism campaign during that time, so in my colleague's eyes, we did no "evangelism."

Another pastor I know makes a big thing about how fast and well his church grows, but that he does no "evangelism."

Believe it or not, in all three cases the word *evangelism* means only a method. All three people cited above mean public meetings and nothing more when they say "evangelism."

Is that all there is to evangelism? What does the word mean, anyway?

Down through the centuries, the word *evangelism* and its derivatives have been used in dozens of different ways to mean just as many different things. The word *evangelize* is actually included in the *New York Times Everyday Reader's Dictionary of Misunderstood, Misused, and Mispronounced Words*. As far back as 1755, Samuel Johnson, the compiler of the *Dictionary of the English Language*, included it as "a word not generally understood."

To understand this issue, we have to trace the use of two words, *evangelism* and *evangelization*, back through church history. At the end, we will attempt a precise definition.

"To all the world in this generation"

In 1886, D. L. Moody, the famous evangelist, called a meeting that resulted in the organization of the Student Volunteer Movement—a movement that lasted into the 1960s. They chose the motto "The Evangelization of the World in This Generation." Sound familiar? Now you know where our own Adventist youth organization got its original name, "Missionary Volunteer Society," and its motto, "The Advent Message to All the World in This Generation."

There is, however, a piece of church history that most people don't know about. Study and research groups at Moody's conference discovered that between A.D. 33 and A.D. 1885, Christians and their churches had proposed two hundred different schemes for world evangelization. All had flopped within ten years of their creation.[1] Since 1886, another one hundred or more schemes have been proposed. All these also folded within ten to twenty years of their creation.

We Adventists have also had innumerable programs and projects geared to evangelism. Most have had a short shelf life. I think part of the problem is that we have never, as far as I can discover, had a precise definition of what we mean by evangelism, though general usage has fixed the idea that evangelism and public meetings are synonymous.[2]

Clues to a definition

The word *evangelism* comes from the Greek word *euongelizein*, which is a combination of two words, *eu*, meaning "good," and *angellein*, meaning to carry news or to proclaim something. That information is not new. We all know that the word *gospel*, a direct derivative of these Greek words, means "the good news." "Good news" is used 132 times in the New Testament, but the word for an evangelist, *euangelistes*, a preacher of good news, only occurs three times, maybe because it was also a title of pagan priests, and the Bible writers were reluctant to use it.[3] In these three instances, Philip (see Acts 21:8) and Timothy (see 2 Timothy 4:5) are called *euangelistes*, and it is mentioned as a specific spiritual gift in Ephesians 4:11.

The word *euangelizo*, which means to *evangelize*, is used twenty-seven times in the New Testament, mostly by Luke and Paul. Luke uses it as a synonym for the proclamation of the good news, and Paul uses it to explain the mission and position of Jesus, who came to bring "good news."

Having waded through all those technical explanations, we can say that in the New Testament, evangelism and its derivatives are used to mean "telling the good news to people who had not heard it before," what we call evangelization. Never in the Bible, however, is the word limited to a methodology or to people with only one spiritual gift.

Add-on or framework?

Is evangelization an integral part of the mission of the church, or is it an add-on to be used occasionally?

According to the Bible, it is not a separate activity among many. Acts 14:7, for instance, gives us a clue by recording that when Paul and his party arrived at a certain place, "they continued to preach the good news." Literally, "they evangelized." It seems that in the early church, evangelizing is simply what the church does. No wonder Ellen White remarks that "the very life of the church depends on her faithfulness in fulfilling the Lord's commission."[4] Evangelization, spreading the good news, is, in fact, the framework of the life of the church.

Does evangelism only mean preaching?

If you will notice carefully, you will observe that your King James Version of the Bible translates every usage of the word *to evangelize* as "to preach." That is one of the reasons we Adventists connect evangelism almost exclusively to public campaigns.

However, in the New Testament, there are more than forty synonyms for the word *evangelize*. They all have the idea of sharing the message, but are not limited to any one method of doing so. One writer comments:

> The New Testament is more dynamic and varied in its modes of expression than we are today. . . . Our almost exclusive use of *preach* for all these synonyms is a sign, not merely of poverty of vocabulary, but of a loss of something which was a living reality in primitive Christianity.[5]

Evangelism, then, in the early church period, was a broad term that took in the whole procedure of presenting the good news to non-Christians and integrating them into the church. It was an application of the great commission.

Notice how the seven biblical cognates of *to evangelize* are connected to the great commission and involve a broad system of evangelization:

To Evangelize Is to

1. Receive (the Holy Spirit)
2. Go (into all the world)
3. Witness (about Jesus)
4. Proclaim (the good news)
5. Disciple (make disciples of all nations)
6. Baptize (people into church fellowship)
7. Train (teach them all things I have commanded)

Three meanings—A.D. 100 to A.D. 1600

For over a thousand years, the word *evangelism* was commonly used by Christian writers in three ways: (1) preaching the gospel; (2) an annunciation, as in the angel Gabriel announcing the birth of Jesus to Mary; and (3) as evangelization, winning people to the Lord, much as we use the word today.

The Protestant Reformation shifts gears

During the Protestant Reformation, the word wasn't used much at all, mostly because the reformers focused their energies on debating Roman Catholics, not on winning souls.[6] Martin Luther, for instance, felt that the great commission was fulfilled by the apostles and did not apply to the church in his day. John Calvin's church in Geneva, Switzerland, sent a mission to France and a feeble mission to Brazil, but it was more commercially oriented than a real ministry.[7]

It wasn't until the 1850s that the meaning of "to spread the gospel" revived. In a book entitled *Evangelism in the Middle of the Nineteenth Century*, Charles Adams, a North American evangelist, applied the word *evangelism* to the entire worldwide missionary enterprise of the church. His view precipitated the widespread use of the word *evangelization* as also referring to the total worldwide task of the church.

Evangelism limited to a methodology

By the turn of the century, however, an interesting shift took place. The word *evangelism* became almost exclusively a term referring to a methodology, mostly due to the writings of a Scottish evangelist named Henry Drummond. He defined evangelism as a three-part methodology, including: (1) the content of the messages preached; (2) the methods of approach to the Western mind; and (3) the types of preaching done in public meetings.[8]

The classic definition

It is evident that the application of the word *evangelism* shifted and bounced according to the use given it by individuals who wrote books or who were popular at a particular moment in history.

In 1918, that changed. In that year a definition appeared that had a lasting effect, even today, on how evangelism is perceived.

A group of Anglican bishops held a conference entitled *The Evangelistic Work of the Church*. As part of the final report, for the first time in 1,900 years, they clearly defined the word *evangelism*:

> To evangelize is so to present Christ Jesus in the power of the Holy Spirit, that men shall come to put their trust in God through Him, to accept Him as their Savior, and serve Him as their Lord in the fellowship of His church.[9]

This definition stuck and has been used over and over again by many churches up to today.

The classical definition and the Adventist Church

Is this a usable definition for us Adventists? Looking at it as a diagram may help.

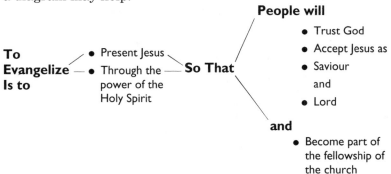

According to this definition, evangelism is a framework, as it were, for the total program of the church. Whatever else the church does, it fits inside the framework of telling people the good news and incorporating them into the church family. A house, for instance, has many rooms, but those rooms are all part of a system of outside walls that sustain a roof. The term *evangelism* is not limited to a methodology. It is wholistic; it is what the church does. Following our analogy, wholistic evangelism is the system of walls; church activities are the rooms.

The church is designed, then, according to the great commission, to win converts, teach them the way of the Lord, offer them a church home for spiritual and social fellowship, and, through the whole system, prepare people for heaven.

Evangelists and witnesses

This brings us to an important distinction and a basic principle. "Evangelists," the people we associate with public campaigns, have a special spiritual gift (see Ephesians 4:11). Not every Christian is called to be an evangelist. Evangelists are given abilities by the Lord to be out on the front line attacking the doctrinal system of the enemy, presenting the truth in a convincing way, and getting decisions from people that those without the gift can never get.

The point is, you do not have to feel guilt if you are not called to be an evangelist. Who gets called to that job is up to the Lord.

On the other hand, every Christian *is called* to be a witness (Acts 1:8). Every Christian falls under the mandate of the great commission. Every Christian can and must learn to give a simple gospel presentation and learn to use the principles of friendship evangelism and other methods. That is the "teaching" part of the great commission. That is where you and I fit into the evangelistic framework of the church.

Hey, that's my church!

The seven churches in Revelation 2 and 3 are unique evidence of the rise and fall of evangelism, as we have defined it in the Christian church. These seven start out as literal churches on the Roman postal road connecting some cities in Asia Minor. Read through each letter, and you will eventually say, "Hey, that's my church."

At the same time, they represent seven eras of church history, each with a distinct application of evangelism.

What blunted evangelism?

Our interest here is to discover what it was that blunted evangelism during an era. Look at the chart below, and you will see that those factors are no strangers to us.

Church	Historical Period	Strong Points	Weak Points That Blunted Evangelism
Ephesus	Early church	Orthodox, persevering, hard working.	Lost its dynamics. See Acts 19.
Smyrna	Postapostolic	Took a lot of flak, heavily persecuted.	None recorded.

Church	Historical Period	Strong Points	Weak Points That Blunted Evangelism
Pergamus	Fourth and fifth centuries	True to the faith.	Doctrinal and lifestyle compromise.
Thyatira	Middle Ages	Love, faith, lots of activity.	Serious lifestyle problems, compromised doctrines, Satan's so-called deep secrets.
Sardis	Reformation	A few true believers hung in there.	Not much truth left. Incomplete deeds.
Philadelphia	Modern era	Kept the faith and did not deny the Word.	None recorded.
Laodicea	Today	None recorded.	Serious need for renewal.

Evangelism is a big word. It describes what the church does and why it exists. Used effectively, it is alive and well on planet Earth.

So how is it with your church? Which church of the seven do you identify with? Does your church have a statement of mission that makes church growth the center of its activities, or is it just hanging in there?

Ask yourself, and your church, these two questions:

1. Using a scale of 1 to 10 (the best), how would you rate *yourself* on a "zeal test"?

2. Using the same scale, how would you rate *your church*?

---

1. David B. Barrett, *Evangelize! A Historical Survey of the Concept* (Birmingham, Ala.: Woman's Missionary Union, 1987).

2. The closest to it is a 1974 Annual Council document that reads, "Evangelism is the communicating of the essential elements of the Gospel of Jesus Christ in the setting of the three angels' messages in such a way as to make possible a response in the hearts of the hearers to accept God's provision of salvation from sin and His provision for victory over sin." From *Evangelism and the Finishing of the Work,* General Conference of Seventh-day Adventists, 1976.

3. Barrett, 11.

4. *The Desire of Ages,* 825.

5. Gerhard Kittel, *Theological Dictionary of the New Testament* (Grand Rapids: Wm. B. Eerdmans Publishing Company, 1965), 3:703.

6. This is another lost piece of church history. While the Reformers were battling the Catholics in Europe, other Catholics were conquering the New World and bringing their missionaries with them. This is why all of the Americas south of the U.S. border are still mostly Roman Catholic today. The truth is that the Catholics did a better job of evangelization than the Protestants of the time. That fact hurts our sensibilities, but if those of us who claim to have the truth don't do the job, somebody else will!

7. G. Baez-Camargo, "The Earliest Protestant Missionary Venture in Latin America," *Church History,* XXI:2, 135-145. If you are interested in studying this subject more, see Kenneth Scott Latourette, "Three Centuries of Advance," in *A History of the Expansion of Christianity* (Grand Rapids: Zondervan Publishing House, 1967), vol. 3.

8. Henry Drummond, *The New Evangelism* (London: Hodder & Stoughton, 1899), 2nd ed.

9. Barrett, 37. The original used *King* instead of *Lord,* reflecting the Anglicans' attachment to the British throne. Most people today replace *King* with *Lord,* a biblical title for Jesus.

CHAPTER 13

Three Angels
Racing the Clock!

Paul and his companion Barnabas found themselves one
Sabbath in a city called Pisidian Antioch in Asia Minor (see Acts
13:14). As was their custom, they went to the synagogue for
church. The ruling elders invited them to speak with these
words: " 'Brothers, *if you have a message* of encouragement for
the people, please speak' " (Acts 13:15, emphasis mine). Maybe
the synagogue leaders recognized Paul's rabbinical credentials
in some way. Synagogues were places where special-interest
groups could voice their opinions, so the opportunity was not
unusual.

The point is that Paul and Barnabas *did* have a message.
They had a very clear and definite message. They knew what
their message was, and they knew how to communicate it. They
had no doubt about their message. They were convinced that
Jewish history led up to a certain point, and that point brought
Jesus of Nazareth, the Messiah. And they had no hesitation
about communicating their message to the congregation.

Paul and Barnabas knew where they were going, they knew
why they were going, and they knew what to do when they got
there, because they knew what their message was.

You cannot do an effective job of evangelization unless you
know, and are convinced of, the message you want to communicate.

The strange case of Ahimaaz
There is a story in the Bible about the strange case of a man

who ran without a message (2 Samuel 15–18).

It happened during Absalom's rebellion. The man was high up in the ranks, the son of the high priest Zadok, and a direct descendent of Aaron. Impressive credentials.

You would assume he knew what he was doing. His father was the principal supporter of David among the priests. Absalom didn't know that, and Zadok and his son Ahimaaz stayed in the capital as spies when David was forced out. The plan was that they would communicate with David, who was hiding out in the desert, and let him know what was going on.

Events moved to Code Red when David was betrayed by some of his inner circle, and Zadok had to find a quick way to get him a message. After a number of adventures, including being stuck in a well overnight hiding out from Absalom's men, Ahimaaz and his friend Jonathan managed to get to David on time and avoid a disastrous ambush.

Shortly after Absalom's and David's forces clashed in battle, Absalom was killed in the famous incident of getting caught in a tree because he refused to get a haircut!

Lacking today's electronic communication networks, runners were the communication system of the times. These runners used a sort of code system. Apparently something about the runner himself indicated the nature of the message. Knowing the news was bad, and that Ahimaaz would be expected to carry only good news, Joab, David's commanding general, elected to send a soldier, apparently a mercenary from North Africa. Seeing him, even at a distance, would let the king know that all was not well and prepare him for the shock of Absalom's death.

Ahimaaz, however, was determined to run anyway. Joab knew that when David recognized him, even at a distance, he would assume everything was OK, simply because Ahimaaz was a well-known and trusted ally. Ahimaaz, however, just wanted to run. He had no message for the king. He just wanted to run. Quick on his feet, he beat the Cushite to where David was waiting for news.

Now here is the point. When he got there, it happened exactly as Joab had figured. David assumed that Ahimaaz had brought good news. He hadn't. He gave David a garbled message that didn't say anything: "I saw great confusion . . . but I don't know what it was" (2 Samuel 18:29). Result? David simply pushed him aside and waited for the next messenger.

Here, again, is the point. You cannot communicate what you don't know. As Ahimaaz found out, there is a principle involved here: *The message must take the person before the person can take the message.*

Ambassadors of a final message

You and I, as Seventh-day Adventists, are called to give a specific, clear, and resounding message to the world. Paul outlines our responsibility clearly in 2 Corinthians 5:17-19:

> Therefore, if anyone is in Christ, he is a new creation; the old has gone, the new has come! All this is from God, who reconciled us to himself through Christ and gave us the ministry of reconciliation: that God was reconciling the world to himself in Christ, not counting men's sins against them. And he has committed to us the message of reconciliation. We are therefore Christ's ambassadors, as though God were making his appeal through us.

We Seventh-day Adventists are heralds of the gospel, the good news of the death, resurrection, ascension, and high-priestly ministry of Jesus. That gospel is the power of God unto salvation (see Romans 1:16). But our message goes beyond that. We are also collaborators with three angels racing the eschatological clock.

Three angels racing the clock

Our message is heralded by three angels racing the clock (see Revelation 14). There are some angels in Revelation who drop down from heaven (see Revelation 18:1), some who stand (see Revelation 7:1), and some who blow trumpets (see Revelation 8:6), but these three angels are at warp speed. They fly! The eschatological clock is ticking.

According to the latest research, the book of Revelation breaks in two, splitting at chapter 15.[1] Events previous to chapter 15 take place before the second coming, during the course of history since the time of Jesus. After chapter 14, the scenes shift to events related to the second coming itself. That leaves chapter 14 as a crossover point between two eras, the era of the church militant, fighting the battle of faith here on earth, and the church triumphant, winning the final victory and reward.

The messages of the three angels form the backbone of Adventism and the prophetic framework of our history as a church. Church pioneer J. N. Andrews gave a concise synopsis of these messages:

> The design of the three great proclamations of this chapter, is, first, to give warning of coming judgment; secondly, to set the people of God upon their watchtower; thirdly, to gather in one body the scattered saints; and, fourthly, to restore the commandments of God to his people, and prepare them for deliverance in the time of trouble, and for translation into his kingdom.[2]

An eternal gospel

The first angel appears on the scene with an eternal gospel to proclaim. An understanding of the Adventist message, and any presentation of it, must begin with the gospel. The power comes from the gospel. It is the good news of Jesus' work of salvation that makes possible everything that follows in these three messages.

A covering of sin encompasses planet Earth, trapping the human race and dooming it to an inevitable fate. The gospel story tells us that Jesus blew a hole in the sin layer. The gospel equips His saints with space suits and jet packs, as it were, and launches them into a new heaven and a new earth where sin will not appear a second time (see Nahum 1:9). Without the gospel rescue mission, the rest of what the angels have to say would be superfluous.

There is only one gospel and one system of salvation. God has not, contrary to popular teaching in many churches, used different methods in different ages.[3] He has used only one (John

3:16). God has made only one covenant with the human race, which is that "all have sinned and fall short of the glory of God, and are justified freely by his grace through the redemption that came by Christ Jesus" (Romans 3:23, 24). That is the everlasting gospel, and that is the beginning point of the Adventist message. Unless the messenger understands, accepts, and lives the gospel, the rest of the messages are only information, not power.

The hour of His judgment

The gospel is power, and it saves, but it is not timeless. That is to say, its presentation is also linked to the final judgment, the point at which the Lord decides that enough is enough and calls a halt to the ravages of sin. The writer to the Hebrews, for instance, says:

> Just as man is destined to die once, and after that to face judgment, so Christ was sacrificed once to take away the sins of many people; and he will appear a second time, not to bear sin, but to bring salvation to those who are waiting for him (Hebrews 9:27, 28).

The message of the first angel introduces a universal call to evangelization based on the urgency of a judgment message whose time has come.

Babylon hits the skids

The second angel slows to subsonic speed long enough to announce the fall of Babylon.

The word *Babylon* is a symbol for the entire complex of the gigantic host of evil powers holding humankind enslaved that we studied about in chapter 3. She has enticed humankind with the "maddening wine of her adulteries" and has almost won.

But not quite! This angel bears the good news that Babylon has had it. This angel hands the saints infrared sensors that pierce the universal fog Babylon has wrapped around the world and lets them see yet three more angels in action (see Revelation 14:14-20). These three do not fly; they fight! One announces the advent of Operation Harvest. The second passes out weapons, and the third punches the Red Button. Babylon never knows what hit her.

Suddenly the wine of Babylon ends up in the "great wine-press of God's wrath" (Revelation 14:19). All the junk she has accumulated for centuries goes into God's trash compactor and gets squished into an insignificant block, dumped on the trash heap of ruin and degradation, and burned to a crisp. And it all happens fast—"one hour," the Bible says (Revelation 18:10).

The second angel in Revelation 14:8 has an urgent message, all right. Get out of Babylon while you still can!

Watching Babylon burn

The third angel makes sure everyone understands just who Babylon is and how she functions, and what the results are if you stick with her.

John and the early Christians were familiar with the way the Roman government dealt with dissenters. The Roman games were popular spectator sports, especially when gladiators fought each other to the death or Christians were thrown to the lions. Sort of like "Monday Night Football" and *Terminator 2* rolled into one.

But here it is different. In this scene, the Christians are in the stands, and Babylon's people are down there in the arena. They are the marked ones this time around. They made everyone drink "maddening wine," but now the tables are turned, and they drink "the wine of God's fury."

There's a difference between wrath and fury. You may get mad, but when you get furious, the fur really starts to fly. The wine of God's fury comes uncut, "full strength," the Bible says. Heaven cuts loose with a kind of napalm unknown in previous history, and Babylon goes down, never to vex the universe again.

A seal and a mark

You and I are involved in this. Yet another angel appears. This one has a seal, called the "seal of the living God" (Revelation 7:2). Seals were the Roman mechanism for marking ownership and signifying authority. This angel seals God's people for time and eternity.

Satan, copying what God does and then giving it his own twist, also marks his people, trying to imitate the seal of God (see Revelation 14:11). Satan, however, has no authority. He cannot seal anything because he has no way of assuring any permanence; he has no word to back him up, because his word is no good. He is a "liar and the father of lies" (John 8:44). As Jesus, who knows him well, says, "When he lies, he speaks his native language" (John 8:44). All he can do is mark some people so they are identified as being on his side.

It's a bad choice, resulting in being tormented with fire and burning sulfur, and a tormenting smoke that rises for ever and ever (see Revelation 14:11).

The messages of the three angels end with a personal appeal:

This calls for patient endurance on the part of the saints who obey God's commandments and remain faithful to Jesus (Revelation 14:12).

Joseph Bates was the first Adventist to see the real doctrinal issue here. He saw the newly arrived seventh-day Sabbath issue as the visible dividing line between the seal and the mark at the end of time.[4] The Sabbath becomes a distinguishing feature because of its significance as a sign of God's authority and the validity and long-lasting effects of His seal.

So here's the message you and I believe and share. Jesus' death at Calvary created an escape mechanism. That is the gospel. The time comes when God will call a halt to the sin issue. That is the message of the first two angels. Both God and Satan clearly identify their people—that is the message of the third angel. If you are on Satan's side, you have had it. That is the message of both the second and the third angels. Those who are on the Lord's side and show it by doctrinal correctness and right living, in the end, win. That is the message of Revelation 14:12.

You and I can choose not to run at all, which in effect puts us right where Satan wants us.

Or we can choose to run without a message, probably doing more harm than good.

Or we can choose to run with a message, which is the only

way to go! As Paul said, "The Lord stood by my side and gave me strength, so that through me the message might be fully proclaimed and all the Gentiles might hear it" (2 Timothy 4:17).

So as we said in the beginning, let's hit the streets, Adventists! The hour of His judgment *is here*. Fix your coordinates on those unchurched friends, relatives, and community members; shoot a laser beam to thaw out the frozen chosen in your congregation; kick it into warp drive; and let's get out there and win some souls before time runs out!

1. For detailed information, see Frank B. Holbrook, *Symposium on Revelation, Books 1 & 2* (Silver Spring, Md.: Biblical Research Institute, General Conference of Seventh-day Adventists, 1992).

2. J. N. Andrews, *Three Messages of Revelation 14* (Nashville: Southern Publishing Association, 1970), iv.

3. This view is called dispensationalism, otherwise known as futurism or the secret rapture. If you are interested in knowing what this system teaches, buy an inexpensive edition of the Scofield Study Bible at a religious bookstore and follow through the chain reference notes.

4. C. Mervyn Maxwell, "Joseph Bates and Seventh-day Adventist Sabbath Theology," in Kenneth A. Strand, ed., *The Sabbath in Scripture and History* (Washington, D.C.: Review and Herald Publishing Association, 1982), 352-363.